Why The Angels Laughed

Eddy Swieson

Why The Angels Laughed

by
Eddy Swieson

Golden Morning Publishing
Winchester, Virginia

Why The Angels Laughed

© 2013 Eddy Swieson   Produced by Richard Choy
Third Printing 2013

Published by *Golden Morning Publishing*
P.O. Box 2697, Winchester, VA 22604

Library of Congress Cataloging-in-Publication Data

Swieson, Eddy
        Why The Angels Laughed

Library of Congress Control Number 2010934540

ISBN 978-1-889283-10-4
        1. Non-fiction—Autobiography—History—Christianity

Printed in the United States by Morris Publishing®
3212 East Highway 30
Kearney, NE 68847
1-800-650-7888

To Rini Tan,

My mother by adoption,

in gratitude for giving

herself in love

Contents

i

Preface To The First Edition

By Mark O. Hatfield
United States Senator from the State of Oregon

I am personally thankful to God for the living reminder that Eddy Swieson is of Christ's healing presence in our world. Eddy's story reminds me once again that the remorse of every biting recollection can be gathered up by the love and healing of Christ, and transformed into gratitude over the joyful memory of His miraculous intervention in all our lives.

Certainly the words of the Apostle Paul ring true in this account of Eddy's pilgrimage: "For the sake of Christ, then, I am content with weakness, insults, hardships, persecutions, and calamities: for when I am weak, then I am strong."

The French writer-politician Andre Malraux has written that "one day it will be realized that men are distinguishable from one another as much by the forms their memories take as by their characters."

Eddy is known by those of us who love him, and now will be more widely distinguished, for the way his memory of the intervention of God in his life proves to him that in his weakness Christ's strength has been made perfect.

I have been reminded once again that what counts in this world is the life of Christ within us breaking, through the alienation and pain, and restoring us to the Father and to one another. For, as I marvel along with Eddy over his miraculous recovery from near-death, from blindness, and crippling illness, to his present healthy life and productive ministry, I marvel as well over the love of God and Christ revealed to all of us in other miraculous ways.

Mark Hatfield
November 1977

Preface To The Second Edition

By Cal Thomas
Syndicated Columnist

I first met Eddy Swieson in 1971 when my wife and I visited Fourth Presbyterian Church in Bethesda, Maryland. He was clearly of Asian descent. His facial construction and black hair, along with his accent, stood out among Fourth's mostly-white congregation. And then he spoke. Actually, he prayed.

I have never heard anyone pray like Eddy. It was as if he actually knew God. I don't mean he knew ABOUT God, but really KNEW Him. I thought I was listening in on a very personal conversation between a father who loved his son, and a son who loved his father. But it was more than that. Eddy's prayer drew me in. He was praying what I would pray if I knew God as he clearly did.

Eddy, along with Pastor Richard Halverson, who would liberate me from religion by introducing me to Jesus Christ, was a contributing factor in our decision to join Fourth, where we remain today under the leadership of the equally magnificent Dr. Robert Norris.

When I read Eddy's fantastic story, I was reminded of the familiar hymn, "Amazing Grace" which contains this verse: "Through many dangers, toils, and snares, I have already come; 'twas grace that brought me safe thus far, and grace will lead me home."

The Grace of God brought Eddy Swieson through a near-death experience as a baby, and then through incredible life circumstances that eventually landed him in America. No human could have had the vision or power to engineer Eddy's life, or make him into the man he is today. It would only have been God's grace.

We Westerners like stories of people who overcome poverty and deprivation. It's part of our cultural history.

But Eddy's life didn't end with his position in what is arguably one of Washington's most powerful pulpits. From Fourth Church, Eddy might have chosen a prestigious college to teach, or acquired a large church pulpit of his own. He might have become an evangelical "star", especially to the growing Asian community in America. He also could have returned to Indonesia or China, and done effective work there. Instead, he chose to be "servant of God" at San Diego International Airport.

It is difficult to relate to this, because such modeling is virtually non-existent in our high profile, narcissistic culture where success – even in evangelical circles – is measured by who you know, how much you have in the bank, the size of your house, the size of your congregation, the car you drive and the clothes you wear.

When I think of Eddy at the airport, helping people with directions or their bags (he has helped me with mine), I think of Philippians 2:5-8 (NIV) where Paul writes: "Your attitude should be the same as Christ Jesus, Who, being in very nature God, did not consider equality with God something to be grasped, but made Himself nothing, taking the very nature of a servant, being made in human likeness." It goes on to say that Jesus "humbled himself and became obedient to death – even death on a cross!"

Eddy would be the first to say how far short he falls when compared to Jesus, but he is more like Jesus than most people I know, including myself.

Jesus said anyone who "wants to become great among you must be your servant" (Matthew 20:26 NIV). Eddy has become a servant of Jesus Christ by serving others, and thus has become great in the only realm that matters: the Kingdom of God.

Those of us privileged to know Eddy, love him because he demonstrates his love for Christ in ways we wish we did. Those who come to know him through reading this marvelous book will want to meet him. If you travel through San Diego International Airport, perhaps you will. Look for him among the servants.

Cal Thomas
February 2010

Foreword To The First Edition

By Howard Norton

Pulitzer Prize-winning Journalist

The angels must have had a good laugh when they learned God's choice to be the future associate pastor of the 150-year-old Fourth Presbyterian Church in Washington, D.C.

It sounds, even now, like a divine practical joke.

For the Lord had put His hand, in 1932, on a tiny Chinese baby; not even a normal healthy baby, but one who was, at the age of three weeks, dying of malnutrition on the floor of a shabby hut in the slum area of a Chinese ghetto near Surabaya, on the island of Java.

Moreover, it was a baby born into Buddhism, to a family with a long tradition of ancestor-worship. And when this story began, the baby's poverty-stricken family was waiting only for the child to breathe its last, to complete preparations for its burial.

Now, forty-five years later, nobody is laughing. It is clear, now, to all who have heard the story, that God, as usual, knew what He was doing. In making His choice, He did it the "hard way" as a dramatic demonstration of the intricate and mysterious manner in which the seemingly disconnected events in our lives can be dovetailed together to accomplish His divine purpose.

For this demonstration the Lord chose the life of Eddy Ie Swieson, the "dying baby" whom He snatched from the gates of death in the Java slum and saved from blindness and crippling illness, from death when the Japanese seized his home village, and then from murder by anti-Chinese rebels.

This book tells the story of the transformation of that dying Buddhist infant into one of America's most distinguished and fruitful servants of Jesus Christ. It is the life story of the man known now to many thousands as Dr. Eddy Ie Swieson, L.Th., D.Min., Bible scholar, linguist, eloquent preacher, and the author of a continuing course of Community Bible Study that has been used in a growing number of cities from coast to coast.

To the large and growing congregation of Washington's enthusiastically evangelical Fourth Presbyterian Church, he is simply "Eddy", their beloved associate pastor.

Howard Norton
November 1977

v

Introduction To The Second Edition

By Eddy Swieson

Radio Broadcaster, Minister, Servant

Due to demands for the book "When the Angels Laughed", which is out of print, I have decided to republish it. Participants of Community Bible Study (which has classes in most major cities around the country) have been asking for the book. Also, inquiries from others who have heard about the book, and how God miraculously rescued me from near-death and dangerous experiences, have influenced my decision to re-publish.

In order to update the readers, I have added an epilogue as well as re-written some of the chapters that have relevancy to my current activities and thinking.

I only wish that Howard Norton, my co-author were here with me to do this. He went to be with the Lord in 1994.

It is my hope that this second edition will help many – those who know me and those who have heard about God's divine intervention in my life. By having the opportunity to read this new edition "Why the Angels Laughed", I hope that you will be blessed and greatly encouraged.

Eddy Swieson
June 2010

Acknowledgements

The Lord has been so gracious, giving me wonderful friends to encourage and assist me in sharing my life story.

The late Howard Norton was the "master-mind" and co-author of this autobiography. When he heard about my near-death experience during infancy, and escape from a massacre during the bloody revolution in Indonesia, and how by the grace of God I came to America and served in the Washington, D.C. area, he urged me to tell my story with his professional expertise.

Senator Mark Hatfield was very supportive and helpful during my early experiences as a young immigrant in this country. Some of the things he did for me are mentioned in this book, and I'm so grateful to have the Senator write the Preface to the first edition.

Cal Thomas, noted news commentator, has always given me great affirmation in my ministry, in a church environment in the past and in the market-place today. On several occasions we have met at San Diego International Airport, where I serve as a volunteer. Indeed, I'm so thankful for his willingness to write the Preface for this second edition.

Leona Choy, a prolific author, contributed much to this revised edition. Not only did she help to refine the manuscript, but she introduced me to Lee Troup, my editor, and guided me in selecting the publisher. Forty-seven years ago when Debbie and I arrived in Washington from Asia, Leona Choy and her late husband, Ted, provided a temporary "home" for us. In God's providence she has again come to assist me.

My thanks to the many other friends who have helped in making this work become a reality. May our good Lord bless each of you.

Eddy Swieson

Chapter 1

Whimpering and Dying Alone

When I was born into a poverty-stricken Chinese family in a slum area of the island of Java, Indonesia (then known as the Dutch East Indies), the world had fallen on hard times. Peoples and governments everywhere seemed to have lost faith in the future, because of dismal failure in the past. Depression was spreading fast. There was not enough work, not enough money, not enough food, not enough medicine; in short, times were bad and getting worse. So, that year, the future was less than promising, even for healthy babies. The year was 1932, the lowest year of the Great Depression. But nobody anywhere in that era of suffering could have had less hope than Eddy Swieson, whimpering and dying alone on a darkened kitchen floor in one of the poor houses in a Chinese ghetto.

My parents, poor and without the skills necessary to earn money, could see no way to keep their new baby alive. So they had decided it would be the kindest thing just to let him die. Their three other children already were suffering the ills of malnutrition. They could not all be saved. So they wrapped little infant, me, just three weeks old, in rags and laid me on the floor of a tiny kitchen adjoining the area where they slept and welcomed relatives. They closed the door because they couldn't bear to listen to my slowly weakening cries. At that point there was a knock on the front door. It was Rini Tan, and although she was my aunt, she was not aware of my existence. Rini, childless because of physical complications, had an overflowing love for children.

What happened next is best told by Rini Tan herself:

I went into the family room and made small talk with my brother-in-law and his wife, Eddy's parents. But I began to notice that every time the conversation stopped for a moment, and there was silence in the room, I could hear a strange, faint, whimpering sound, like a kitten that wants to get back in out of the yard.

This happened again and again, and it seemed that the sound was coming from an adjoining room. Finally, I got so curious that I just got up and walked over to the door of the room where the sound was coming from. When I opened it, all I could see in the semi-darkness was a little bundle of rags on the floor. I moved closer, and thought I saw a slight movement from inside the bundle. Again I heard that faint whimpering sound from inside the bundle.

2

I knelt on the floor and pulled aside the rag, half-expecting to find a kitten inside. But, I was surprised – yes, shocked – to find instead a newborn baby! Nobody had told me that there was a new member of the family. It was obvious, even there in the dark, that this baby was very, very sick. He was nothing but skin and bones. His tiny stomach was bloated from starvation, but even then it wasn't any bigger than a tennis ball. He looked so fragile and so sick that I was afraid to touch him. So I rose and hurried back into the family room.

"Where did this baby come from?" I asked, though the question sounded foolish. "Nobody told me that you had a child! Why didn't you tell me? Don't you know he is almost dead now? Why aren't you doing something? This is callous and cruel! You must not let him die."

Anger and fear for the baby rose within me, and I scolded the parents in words that I would not like to repeat. They just sat there and shook their heads helplessly, while I continued my tirade. Finally, when I gave them a chance to speak, they confessed to me, reluctantly and with a show of shame, that there was no money for a doctor, in fact, no money for food or anything else.

Well, that cooled my temper tantrum, and I spoke to them in kinder tones. I didn't even wait for permission. I just strode back into that darkened room, and knelt beside the pile of rags. Baby Eddy was so fragile that I just didn't dare to pick him up, fearing I might break one of his tiny bones. So I went to the bedroom, borrowed a small pillow, put it on the floor beside Eddy, and literally scooped him and rolled him onto the pillow without actually lifting him from the floor. With Eddy and the pillow in my arms, I rushed off to the clinic in our little suburban town of Mojokerto.

I didn't really expect to get much help, even from the clinic, because Eddy was so far gone, and our grubby little clinic was not the kind of place you would expect to find a reputable doctor. But I didn't realize at that time – I was then a practicing Buddhist – that the Lord Jesus Christ was using me to accomplish His purpose, which was to save Eddy for service to the body of Christ.

Well, I rushed through the door of the clinic and looked hurriedly about the outer office for someone who could help me. There was no one in sight. But as I turned around, a young Dutchman came through the door. Since he was wearing a stethoscope around his neck, I took it for granted that he was a doctor. Before he could open his mouth, I was pouring out the whole story about how I had found this starving baby on the floor, and that I was afraid the baby was dying. Would he please do something, quick!

The doctor nodded, and without a word, took the pillow and the baby into his arms and entered a nearby office. Only then did I notice he was wearing a small nameplate, which announced that he was Dr. Weese.

I looked him over rather sharply, because it seemed to me that he was awfully young to be a real doctor – too young, to be a good doctor, anyway. And while he examined Eddy, I plied him with questions.

Little by little, as he examined Eddy from head to toe, his story came out. Dr. Weese was just out of medical school, and had come from Holland to serve his internship at this terrible, rundown clinic. Then the miraculous news! His specialty, he said, was pediatrics; he specialized in taking care of children. And this baby, my own little Eddy, was his very first patient as a

4

practicing pediatrician!

Well, I couldn't decide whether to be nervous over the fact that he was such a new doctor, or to be happy that taking care of babies was the work he was trained to do. So I decided that I could be both nervous and happy at the same time. His next words gave me my first bit of hope that Eddy might, after all, have a chance to live.

"This baby is my first patient," he said, "and I cannot, I will not, start my medical career by losing my first patient. So I promise you," he said, turning and looking straight into my eyes, "that this baby is not going to die! This baby is going to live!"

That made me feel a little better, but I stayed there in the clinic with Eddy most of that first day and far into the night. I wanted to make sure this young man was, indeed, what he said he was. It turned out that he was even more than he claimed to be. He was not only a doctor, but a man of infinite compassion. That first night he was right beside his tiny patient almost until dawn. And when I returned to the clinic early the next day his eyes were heavy from lack of sleep. So I told him that I would watch the baby for a while, and urged him to take a nap, which he reluctantly did.

For over three months – for 100 days, to be exact – that's the way it went. Dr. Weese grappled with death, and tiny Eddy clung precariously to life. Gradually, toward the end of February 1933, the improvement in Eddy became so marked that even in my moments of deepest pessimism, I could not deny that the doctor was winning his first big battle.

Then came that happy day when the doctor greeted me with a victorious smile as I entered the clinic for my morning visit. "I think he's strong enough, now,"

he said. "you may take him home, if you will promise to
do what I tell you, and not make him sick again by
giving him foods that are too rich, or spoil him and
make him a crybaby by too much attention." The doctor
flashed his boyish grin after that remark. It was obvious
to me, at that moment, that the doctor loved Eddy, too,
as I did. And that it was not only pride in his success
with his first patient that brought tears to his eyes when
I wrapped Eddy in a blanket and started toward the
door. He was going to miss this tiny life that he had
saved. I turned to wave a final goodbye as we reached
the dispensary door, but Dr. Weese already had turned
his back and was rubbing one of his eyes with the
corner of a handkerchief, complaining about "the dust"
that was always blowing into the building when the
doors were opened. I looked around, but there was no
cloud of dust that I could see!

Now three months had passed since I found Eddy
dying on the floor of my brother-in-law's rundown home.
In those three months, Eddy had become my own child,
and my love for him could not have been any greater if
he had been born to me.

I knew he was going to need constant care, but it
never seemed like a burden to me. I honestly thought of
it as a privilege. I knew I could never have a child of my
own flesh. But Eddy, the child of my brother-in-law and
sister was, in a very real sense, a child of my own flesh –
my father was his grandfather, just as it would have
been had Eddy been born of a union of my husband and
myself. I felt strongly that Eddy was mine because I had
helped to save his life; because there would be no Eddy
if I had not snatched him from his natural parents. So I
vowed solemnly that I would never allow anyone to take
Eddy from me. I determined, to make this adoption
legal, if that were possible, even if it took my whole life

to do it. I had no idea, at the time, how nearly accurate was my estimate of the length of time it would take to achieve my goal of legal adoption.

Not long afterward, the young doctor came to my home for a visit, to check up on Eddy's health. As we sat in the parlor I could see that he had a problem on his mind, so I made small talk and waited for him to say what he had in mind... Finally he did get to the point.

"My wife and children," he said, "are returning to Holland soon. I have been giving this a lot of thought, knowing how much you love Eddy. But I wonder if you love him enough to give him up, for the sake of his own future. I wonder if you love him enough to let me send him to Europe with my family. He can get a good European education there, and make something of himself. I have a deep conviction that this little boy has talents that he should be given a chance to develop. I am sure you have sensed that I have a very deep affection for him, and would gladly adopt him and bring him up as my own son. Please sleep on this. Don't decide right now. Think it over. There is time. I think you will decide that in Europe he would have a better chance in life. And I'm sure you would have many chances to see him as he grows to manhood."

I knew in my heart that this moment would come, but still was not prepared for it. Many times I had told myself that if the doctor or anyone else ever asked me to give up Eddy, I would turn them down flat. But now, I found myself wavering. The very thought of giving up "my son" tore my heart, but I knew the doctor was right, that Eddy's chances in life would improve with European training. So, after a few moments of silence, I heard myself tell the doctor that I would indeed think it over. We shook hands, and he departed.

That night, and for many nights, I wrestled with the issue. What could I offer him? Only a mother's love. I prayed before my ancestors and asked their advice. I sat through many hours of Buddhist meditation. But it was not until almost the eve of the departure of the doctor's family that I came to a decision.

"Dr. Weese," I said, "you are a kind and compassionate man. I am forever in your debt. But I think that Eddy needs a mother's love more than anything else, and that I need Eddy as much as he needs me. You have done wonderful work, and I will pray that the great Buddha will reward you richly, but I have decided to keep Eddy here with me."

So the doctor's family left for Europe. Months later, we heard a report that the ship on which they traveled had never reached Holland, and had probably run into a severe storm and capsized, with the loss of all on board. Although the report was never confirmed (the doctor himself had moved to another city), I went to the temple to thank the great Buddha and burn incense on his altar, as I was convinced that he had put in my heart to keep Eddy with me in Java.

Years later, after becoming a Christian, I came to realize that Buddha had nothing to do with that decision. It was Jesus Christ who had planted that love in my heart, and the Lord who led me to make the right decision, even though I was the follower of a pagan religion at that time. The Lord does, indeed, work in mysterious ways! ☩

Chapter 2

A Most Painful Time In My Life

I did my best to be a normal, mischievous boy for my first eight years, although always seeming to be just getting over, or just coming down with some illness. From what my foster mother told me about my shaky start in life, I considered myself lucky to be alive, even though physically weak. Any boyish fun I could manage was a welcome bonus, along with the gift of life itself.

My mother was a no-nonsense disciplinarian, the kind that the Bible applauds. In spite of my constantly frail state of health, I knew that I was risking some stinging corporal punishment every time I violated the parental precepts. One of the best-enforced rules of my childhood was that I must never under any circumstances smoke anything: cigarettes, cigars, pipe, dried grass, tobacco, corn silk, or anything else. Now any eight-year-old boy will tell you that a parental order so strict and absolute presents a challenge that no one can resist. That was the way it looked to me, anyway.

The big chance for some illicit smoking came to my "social set" every time there was a wedding. And there were a lot of weddings, because the Chinese residents of Java tended to have big families. We would dress up in our best, like good little boys, and move around obediently among the wedding guests. Then, taking care that nobody was watching, we would snatch a cigarette or cigar, and stuff it into a pocket. To us, it didn't matter that the illicit bit of tobacco might already have been half smoked and discarded, although we did prefer the unused cigarettes and cigars.

When we had grabbed enough of them to give everyone a few puffs, we would disappear, one at a time, and reassemble in the woodshed or some other outbuilding out of sight from the main house, to experiment with the smoking materials we had filched.

Despite the precarious state of my health, I smoked right along with the healthiest of them until my head began to spin and my breath smelled like the inside of a chimney that needed sweeping. Inevitably, my mother charged me with "the crime", and every time I opened my mouth to lie about it, I breathed a distinct air of guilt in her face. My mother, without speaking a word of disapproval, always went to the corner of the kitchen where she kept a piece of stout rattan, and gave me a lesson on the wages of the sin of disobedience.

There were other kinds of illicit fun interspersed with spells of illness during this quiet, but physically painful time of my life. There was, for example, the "banana parade" game. It was easy to play, and we all thought it uproariously funny. We would sit on a roadside bench, and watch the older girls promenade up and down the street in the evening in their fancy clothes. As the evening shadows began to fall, the game was to eat the bananas we had brought along, then carefully toss the skins into the street where the girls were walking in their wooden-soled slippers. As masters of the sport, we knew exactly what would happen when one of those wooden soles stepped on a banana skin. The result was instantaneous and dramatic. It never failed.

Thinking back over the years, I don't think my mother ever found out what we were doing out there in the early evenings, so I was never punished for it. Hopefully the young ladies who were our embarrassed victims have found it in their hearts by now to forgive us!

The end of this period of boyish fun and games came about 1940, just before the Japanese entered World War II. Despite my mother's best efforts, I became more and more anemic and my health began to decline alarmingly.

Now Rini Tan, my "mother", had taken some training as a nurse, and she knew a bit about the basics of modern medicine and the science of nutrition. She developed some ingenious substitutes for the remedies we were unable to purchase on the open market.

To strengthen the bones in my spindly legs and arms, for example, she bought from the villagers buckets of natural lime. Then she put it into a large earthen jar, filled with water until all the lime had settled to its bottom and a large part of it had been dissolved. Dipping the clear limewater from the top of the jar she forced me to drink it, day after day and month after month. To my surprise it worked. There's nothing weak and spindly now about my arms and legs.

But I was weak and needed vitamin B, which

wasn't available anywhere in Java at the time. Again my mother proved equal to the challenge. She searched for, and finally found supply of rice husks which, she said, contained some of the most effective nutrients in the rice plant. She ground the husks into a powder, added some sugar and water and other things I cannot recall, and when the mixture was completed she pronounced it vitamin B. Now whether this mixture had any of the properties of vitamin B, I'm not in a position to say, but I do know that it worked just as effectively on my weakened body as the limewater had worked on my little bones.

I began to regain my strength, and my hope of being strong enough to go back to school increased. Having missed years of school because of my precarious state of health, I truly wanted to go to school. I loved to study and really enjoyed my time as a student in the Dutch Elementary School.

But just as I seemed strong enough to go back to the classroom, I was laid low again by a new sickness, malaria. It was difficult to get quinine to ease the attacks of malaria, so my mother turned to the artificial quinine called Atabrine, a remedy well known to American veterans of the war in the South Pacific. It was a bitter-tasting pill, and after constant dosage turned the skin from its natural tone to a sickly yellowish.

Along with the attacks of malaria came spells of pleurisy, pneumonia and stomach disorders. My stomach, in fact, suffered continually from the crude substitute medicines. Even though they did prove effective, they were hard to take, and there were some unfortunate side effects. The limewater, for example, was extremely bitter and made me sick for an hour or so, every time I drank it – which was almost every day.

Malaria attacks came about every month, and every attack left me weaker. I fell ill more frequently with the maladies that accompanied the malaria. The most alarming thing in my life started about this time. My eyesight began to fail, probably as the result of the medicines I had been taking. For two years I was nearly blind, and that shattered my hope of returning to school. But in spite of my sickness and extremely weak condition, my mind remained alert, and I longed to get back to my studies.

My mother fought desperately to bring me back to health, especially after I began to go blind. So she consulted the local "dukun," a Javanese witch doctor supposed to have the power to chase out the evil spirits that caused the illness. Her method – our "dukun" was a woman – was to get the evil spirits out of the house where they would not have such a close-range shot. So she would go into a sort of dance through the house and around it on the outside - a dance of exorcism – and she would chew up a mouthful of foul-smelling herbs and spit them all over the place as she danced. Then she would collect her fee and depart.

The spirits that were "guests" in our home must have found it too comfortable to give up, for the witch doctor's efforts didn't seem to do me any good. But we followed her directions to the letter. She had advised us to hold a full-moon festival – a "selamatan" – every month to keep the spirits happy. It was a very expensive brand of preventive medicine, because the festivals were elaborate, but we took no chances. They were held every month while I was ill, and even afterward, just in case of a relapse.

One awful day, I fell from a moving vehicle as it bounced across some railroad tracks, and was unconscious for several hours. When I finally opened my eyes, my first sight was this ugly "dukun" dancing around me and spitting all over me from her mouthful of

13

stinking herbs. My worried mother was standing by, wringing her hands and crying. As I opened my eyes and asked what had happened, the "dukun" gave a whoop of victory, broke off the spitting, and collected her fee. She was gone almost before I could scramble to my feet.

By now I was years behind children of my age, but my health began to improve. The malarial attacks came less often, and finally the great day came. I returned to the classroom, eager to catch up with those who had been fortunate enough to stay in school.

I studied night and day, and was moving up fast when I encountered an unexpected barrier: the Japanese, who struck Pearl Harbor on December 7, 1941, swept southward through the Philippines and attacked the island of Java where we lived. My foster father, who for years had operated a prosperous trucking business, was put out of business when the Japanese seized his trucks. So our family support fell to my mother, who was the proprietor of a small factory making handmade native Javanese fabrics.

My attendance at school became spotty after the attack by the Japanese. Whether we attended or stayed home depended on the location of the day's fighting. So, from the time of the initial Japanese attack, until quiet was restored by the Japanese occupying forces, attending school became only a sometime thing. Fortunately for my education, the Japanese made quick work of the task of overwhelming the Dutch forces that were defending the island at the time of the 1942 assault. But, for a 10-year-old boy, the war was the most excitement ever witnessed in his brief span of life. Secretly, I hoped the fighting would go on for a long time. The thought of danger never entered my mind!✟

Chapter 3

War and Revolution

The top of a cherry tree looked like a great place to sit and watch the war. At 10, I loved the action. It didn't occur to me that there was any real danger, or that people were being killed, or that my own family might be next on the list of fatalities.

There were a few minor irritations. I still remember my father's livid outrage when the Japanese forces seized his trucks, leaving him without any way to support the family. And even my mother, who was normally a kindly, even-tempered woman, used expressions I did not realize were in her vocabulary when Japanese soldiers ransacked our house and took our supply of food.

But we were not seriously inconvenienced by these acts of war. My parents were canny enough to foresee each crisis, so we had hidden resources the

Japanese never found, and we never suffered any real hunger. Schools were closed during the initial assault early in 1942. This was a blessing to me, because I had the opportunity to watch the fighter planes in action from the top of our cherry tree. And what a show, for the short time it lasted! Fighter planes streaked overhead, diving toward targets that were just out of sight from my perch. I would watch them flash by, then listen for the rattle of machine gun fire and the dull thud of exploding bombs. It was just like the movies, only really happening. What could be more fun?

Then, one day, as I climbed down from my perch, the war got too close to be fun. As I was just about to go into the house, I heard gunfire close by. This was too good to miss, I thought, so I turned and started back toward the cherry tree. My mother, pale with fright, rushed from the house, grabbed my arms, pulled me back inside, and pushed me flat on the floor.

Suddenly, we could hear bullets striking the wall. We hugged the floor, trying to make ourselves as flat as the mats that covered it. We waited and waited for what seemed to be hours, motionless and quiet. At last, my mother rose, and I got up, too. Only then did we see how close death had come. Along one wall of the room where we had taken refuge there was a neat line of bullet holes, about three feet above the floor. Standing, we would have been hit, possibly killed. Once again, God had provided a miraculous escape. And once again Buddha got the credit, along with our ancestral spirits. My mother dutifully went to the temple and made offering to the spirits.

Then came chilling news. My maternal grandfather was seized by the Japanese MPs. He was taken to a concentration camp, tied to a tree and beaten, and later starved to the point of collapse. He told us that they ridiculed him and kicked him between beatings. His house was confiscated, and converted into an emergency station where the wounded were brought. The trees, every day, were decorated with hanging human bodies, hoisted high to ease the stench. Two or three times a week the soldiers would cut them down, stack them like firewood, douse them with gasoline and burn them. That was the only funeral they got.

We heard via the "grapevine" that the jails were not too bad. Not crowded at all, our informants said, because the Japanese were using an efficient method of weeding out the excess prisoners - they were shooting them. But there was evidence of great cruelty. We saw many bodies unspeakably mutilated.

One day the soldiers rounded up all the local residents they could find and herded them into a park. They had caught 10 alleged thieves. When we arrived on the scene under escort, the thieves had been tied to separate poles and stripped of their clothes. After the soldiers were satisfied with the size of the audience, 10 MPs stepped forward with pistols loaded, and each stood before a separate victim and pumped three bullets into the bodies.

These moments were frightening, but we were fortunate. The shooting did discourage the stealing, but the news passed from neighbor to neighbor told of scores of atrocities. Women were attacked and then murdered. Property was stolen, householders tortured in their own homes, then tied to their furniture and cremated when the house was put to the torch. But aside from my grandfather's painful experience, no one in our family was seriously hurt.

Food was scarce and we were using corn and tapioca as substitutes for the rice that was our usual diet. We had to take good care of our clothes, because there was no clothing to buy. There were no medicines for the sick. And, as usual, I was sick; not just once, but often.

When the Japanese finally surrendered in 1945, we rejoiced that peace had returned, but it had not. Immediately, there was a fierce and bloody revolution against the Dutch rule of the Islands, led by the late Mr. Sukarno. This was much worse than the Japanese invasion – at least for the Chinese – because the revolutionaries suspected the Chinese of being pro-Dutch. It was a time of torture and death for many of our friends, an anti-Chinese massacre.

Every morning human bodies floated down the river past our house, most of them with bamboo sticks piercing their chests or stomachs, and many with heads missing, or hands and feet chopped off by torturers. Our trucks were seized again, by the revolutionaries. My worried father grew ill tempered and battled frequently with my mother. After every major domestic battle, my mother would grab her belongings and take me by the arm to my grandparents' house, to stay for as long as two months.

It was during one of our sudden visits to my grandparents that we had one of our closest escapes. Every day someone we knew was being killed, so we stayed indoors as much as possible. Early one evening, while my cousin and I were studying in our room, there was a crashing sound as two terrorist gunmen broke down our front door and rushed into the house with guns cocked and pointed at us. They rounded up the whole family and took us into the living room, while they started a search of the premises.

Grandpa, who was nearly blind, was trembling with outrage. To the horror of all the rest of us, he decided to frighten them out of the house by shouting at them, and threatening to have each one of the terrorists executed by a firing squad – though we couldn't imagine how he expected that this would scare them, since he had no firing squad under his command. He had only his family.

We were frozen with fright, certain he would anger them and they would shoot us. But grandpa kept on yelling, and amazingly the ruffians went out the door hurriedly and took to their heels. As soon as they left, we ran to the back porch to rebuild our courage, and saw another pair of gunmen beating our servants. They had apparently been sent to the rear to guard the house and prevent our escape. But when they saw us running free, and their own colleagues in a running retreat, they grabbed their guns and fled, too!

Well, grandpa was the family hero that day. "All you have to do is scare them," he said in a tone of authority. "You see how easily they frighten."

We were terrified, but my grandfather was equal to every occasion. He assembled us in the dining room for a lecture on self-defense. "Next time, you cowards," he said, "do something to scare them. Don't leave it all to me. Here's what we will do. Get a lot of broken glasses and all the other broken glass things you can find, and put them on top of every tall cabinet in the house and tie strings to the piles atop each cabinet. If these outlaws come again, just pull the strings and make all those glasses crash to the floor at the same time. That will get rid of them."

We looked at each other, but nobody could think up a better plan, so we dutifully gathered broken glassware and set the traps. Every night for several days, before we went to bed, we took turns checking our booby traps. Finally, in broad daylight, when we least expected them, there was another terrorist attack on our house. A glance out of the window made it clear that they had us surrounded. All of them had guns, pistols, even a submachine gun. Two of them came in, jumped on my grandfather's secretary in the office, and broke open the safe. They took what they wanted, and left. Not until they were all gone did any of us remember that we had not pulled the glassware down from the cabinets to frighten them. Grandpa was furious!

One morning, a short time later, I was working on my bicycle in front of the house, when I heard something that sounded like firecrackers. I stood on my bench and could see about half a dozen men in black uniform and black beret, surrounding the house directly across the street. They were the commandos – composed of pro-Dutch natives. As they began firing at the house, there were answering shots from inside the house. I dropped to the ground quickly, and crawled to a nearby bush to watch the battle, just yards away. I was frozen with fear that they would come next to our house. Now and then there was a human scream from inside. Later we learned they had trapped a group of terrorists in the house and wiped them out.

As my "military expertise" grew, from watching these skirmishes, I took mental note that having a squad of fearless fighters – like those commandos – scout quietly on foot was a more efficient and successful way to eliminate the enemy than to call a truckload of soldiers accompanied by tanks and other noisy equipment, as was frequently done. The noise of the tanks and the trucks always tipped off the terrorists that they were being stalked, so they usually got away. The commandos were clever to use silence and surprise. When I join the army, I thought, I will remember this skillful method.

The terrorist tactics were to sneak into a private home, and open fire on the Dutch troops who patrolled the streets. It was tough on the families who lived in and were forced to stay in those houses during the battle. Many died.

Often, when a Dutch trooper entered a private home during the day, where the terrorists were in hiding, they would make that home a target the same night. They were known to gun down all the women and children in the house, and then torture the head of the house to death. This was to discourage local residents from cooperating with the beleaguered Dutch regime.

Sometimes terrorists, disguised as sellers of fruits and vegetables or rice, would pass along the street and visit each house. Before leaving they would slip a note to the householder demanding that he place a gallon of gasoline in a convenient spot, to be picked up by them the same night. The gasoline was to be used to manufacture Molotov cocktails. When we were given such notes, there was nothing to do but comply. To refuse was death. On the other hand, if the Dutch military had caught us providing gasoline to the rebels, the punishment also was severe. It was a time of genuine terror. And we did not wonder when we saw daily truckloads of human bodies being hauled away to be burned. We knew why they had been killed, and we wept for them.

There was also constant danger of terrorists looting private homes. It was the Chinese – because they controlled the island's economies – who were victims of the worst looting. Often burning the home followed the looting, and those families who were allowed to leave the houses before they were set fire considered themselves lucky.

The home of my paternal grandparents was one

of the many that were destroyed by fire. Because of the looting and the burning, it was common practice for a family to bury its jewelry and other valuables in the ground, leaving no marker to give away the hiding place. When the revolution ended, after four long years, many families had great difficulty finding their valuables, having forgotten where they were buried.

The Sukarno revolution finally ended, but to us who were young it seemed endless. There had been seven years of constant war between the outbreak of fighting in World War II in 1942 and the end of the revolution in 1949.

We had become hardened to the sight of bodies drenched with blood. After spending hours hiding under beds and other furniture, we were never surprised to find the streets littered with bodies of humans and animals, waiting to be carted away.

Looking back now, as an adult, and realizing the terrible dangers that surrounded us during both the war and the revolution, it was only through God's infinite mercy that we did not lose a single member of our family through all of those nightmarish seven years.

For the Japanese, Indonesia was the richest prize of World War II. They had to seize it quickly, because it was the closest major source of oil. And without oil, their whole war machine would collapse. So they rushed southward while Pearl Harbor was still burning, and made quick work of wiping out the tiny Dutch force that was defending the islands. The Japanese Navy was pumping oil from the fast-flowing wells of Borneo, while the assault on Java and Sumatra was still under way. Oil that flowed from some of the wells was so free of pollutants that it could be used to fire ship's boilers without refining.

It was Indonesia that kept the Japanese factories supplied with tin, copper, rubber, lumber, bauxite and nickel for the three years that the Japanese military ruled the islands. Strangely, there was scarcely any sign of resentment among the native Indonesians over this snatching of their natural resources by an invading enemy. But the Japanese had studied history, and had sent scouts among the islands of Indonesia for years before the war. They saw a unique opportunity to grab the wealth of the Indonesian islands, while at the same time winning the friendship and support of the Indonesian natives and their leaders. Here's how they did it.

For almost 100 years before the outbreak of World War II, there had been a rising flow of immigrants from China to Indonesia. They came from the overcrowded provinces of Kwangtung, Fukien and Kwangsi Chuang, in search of jobs on the newly formed plantations in the mid-19th century, dazzled by the promise of a better life on these rich islands. Then the Dutch rulers discovered the mineral wealth of the islands, and the Chinese came to get the high pay (by Chinese standard) that the new mine owners were giving to attract miners. By the early 20th century, the Chinese were coming by the hundreds of thousands. There were so many, that the Dutch government of the islands slammed the door against all further immigration from China. But in a country made up of more than 3000 islands, how could the door be closed? The Chinese population kept on increasing. There simply were not enough border guards to watch the vast miles of shoreline. The "wetback" Chinese rowed or swam ashore at night from the hundreds of colorful junks that sailed silently among the islands, ostensibly as trading ships. It was not until the Great Depression of the 1930s eliminated the demand for labor that the flow of Chinese immigrants slowed and then stopped. Some of the immigrants returned to China, but the 80 or 90 years of Chinese immigration gave Indonesia a permanent population of more than 2,000,000 Chinese, hundreds of thousands already Indonesian citizens by birth. Since the Chinese tend to have big families, their numbers on the islands continued to grow until in 2010 there are an estimated 4,000,000 Chinese there, most of them born on the islands.

Now the Chinese since ancient times, like the Jews and the Indians, have remarkable talents for business. So when the job market evaporated in the Indonesian islands they turned to their inherited talents. Barred by colonial law from buying or owning farmland, they became shopkeepers, moneylenders, bankers, wholesale merchants, exporters, importers, shippers, factory owners, technicians, and artisans. And before the 150 million Indonesians realized what was happening, the four million Chinese in their midst had gained a firm control of the whole Indonesian economy.

Human nature seems to resent an inflow of foreigners, especially when those foreigners are as clannish as the Chinese, and even more so when they are so successful that they take the local economy away from the natives.

By the outbreak of World War II, resentment of the Chinese domination of Indonesia's economy was running high among the natives. So when the Japanese loosed their blitz and snatched the wealth of Indonesia from the owners, it was the Dutch and the four million Chinese who suffered most, not the 150 million native Indonesians, most of whom were farmers and workers.

That began decades of discrimination and suspicion against the Chinese in Indonesia.
Native political leaders, including Sukarno and Suharto, two of the future leaders of the country, willingly cooperated with the Japanese invaders. It was the Chinese and the Dutch who came under suspicion and were searched and harassed by the Japanese, because they were the ones who had lost the most in the invasion, and seemed the most likely to retaliate.

Then, three days after the Japanese surrendered on August 17, 1945, the pro-communist Sukarno launched his revolution, and the whole round of property seizure and harassment of the Chinese and Dutch began all over again. This lasted another four years, until 1949, when Indonesia won its independence from Holland.

The arrival of peace in 1949 brought even more troubles to the Indonesian Chinese. The destruction of the Indonesian economy, caused by the war, was made worse by the peace. The victorious Sukarno clamped a dictatorial "guided democracy" on the Indonesian state. A strict system of foreign exchange controls virtually trapped the Indonesian population on their individual islands. It eliminated almost all chance for foreign travel.

Import and export controls killed off much of Indonesia's booming foreign trade, building up a mountainous trade deficit, and an even more bigger national debt. Control of shipping restricted movement even between the islands, some of which were under rebel factions and in a state of war. There was censorship of the mails, the telegraph, and the telephone systems. Sukarno's spies were everywhere. Missionary work among the islands was at a near standstill because of the paralysis of internal life under the communist-tinted "guided democracy" of Sukarno.

Indonesia had been a glittering temptation to exploiters, conquerors and colonialists throughout history. When Christopher Columbus accidentally discovered America in 1492, he was disappointed because it blocked what he had hoped was a shorter route to Indonesia. Even in Columbus' day, Indonesia had been enjoying a high level of civilization for more than a 1000 years. The people now known as Indonesians are the product of intermarriage of several different groups of Asians who ruled the islands over the centuries.

The Buddhist kingdom of Srivijaya, from the 7th to the 12th century, ruled the islands now known as Indonesia and much of the rest of southeastern Asia from a capital established on Sumatra. In the 14th century the Hindu kingdom of Majapahit dominated the same geographical region from a capital in Eastern Java.

These two early kingdoms have given the Indonesians a legacy of temples and other ancient structures that rank among the world's finest examples of ancient art. They also had an important influence on the physical and other characteristics of what we now call the native Indonesians.

Islam started to infiltrate the islands in the 12th century and has now replaced Hinduism in all the islands except Bali. Today, 80% of the Indonesians are professing Muslims, 16% are Christians – about half of them Roman Catholics – and the rest a scattering of Hindus, Buddhist, Confucianists and others.

The Portuguese arrived in the 16th century and established trading posts. By this time the once-powerful Indonesian kingdoms had been broken up into small states that were unable to stand up against

Western colonial incursions. The Dutch began arriving in 1602, quickly took over colonial rule of all the Indonesian islands, and kept the control for most of the next 300 years.

The British snatched control from the Dutch briefly, during the Napoleonic period in Europe. With the fall of Napoleon, the Dutch resumed control and developed Indonesia – with the help of a few hard-working Chinese – into one of the world's richest colonial possessions.

Agitation for independence got under way in Indonesia in the early 20th century, led by small group of young professional men and students, most of them educated in the Netherlands. A number of the leaders of the country, including Sukarno, were imprisoned by the Dutch for long periods, for their political activity.

For 10 years after Indonesia got its independence in 1949, the country was politically fragmented among a large number of small parties, with a long succession of short-lived national governments. In 1957 a succession of rebellions in Sumatra, Sulawesi and other islands so discredited the parliamentary system that Sukarno met little opposition, when   he set himself up as a strong independent executive in 1959, and aligned the country's foreign policy with the Asian communist states.

Only the Indonesian Army remained outside Sukarno's absolute control. By 1965 evidence of mismanagement and misconduct by the Sukarno regime became overwhelming. When the Indonesian communist party then attempted to prevent the loss of its power by murdering several top generals of the army, General Suharto was able to defeat the coup by force of arms and forced Sukarno to hand over to him political and military power in 1966. Sukarno remained for a time as a figurehead president, but was voted out of office by the People's Consultative Assembly in 1967, and went into retirement until his death in 1970.

General Suharto, elected to a full five-year term as president in 1968, won the respect and admiration of the country for his moderation, and was re-elected in 1973. Under Suharto, Indonesia turned its back on ideological extremes, and set as its priority goals the economic rehabilitation of the country and improvement of the living standards of the people. The domestic and international economic and financial ruins left by the Japanese, and by Sukarno and his communist-backed regime, will not likely be wiped out entirely for decades.✟

Chapter 4

A Surge of Unutterable Joy

There's a special kind of fear that goes with
Buddhism. I was haunted by it as a boy of 17, about to
graduate from high school. It wasn't death that I feared
so much as life; specifically, the life that I believed
would come after death. After 17 years of almost
continuous illness, I was beginning to feel pretty good. I
wanted to get through to some kind of higher power, to
convince Him that I deserved some years of enjoyment
before having to take my chances on the next life. Full of
self-pity, I was afraid the Almighty, whoever He was,
might not have heard of my hard life, and might order
me reincarnated as one of the lower animals in the next
life. For I firmly believed in the Buddhist "wheel of life"
doctrine – that we all have to be reincarnated numerous
times, and in many different forms of life. My
nightmares were about coming back to life as a stray
dog or a cricket.

It was about this time that a Dutch friend gave me a copy of the New Testament in the Dutch language. Dutch and Indonesian were my only languages then. I thanked him profusely, like a true Asian, and put it in my pocket. Arriving home, I put it on the top shelf with some of my last year's schoolbooks, without even opening it. That shelf was my discard pile.

I used to lie in bed and look out the window at the big, tropical Indonesian moon, and wonder what the future had in store for me. The more I wondered, the greater my worry. And the more I worried the greater my depression, until I wept into my pillow without really knowing why.

As the only son of my foster parents, I knew what was expected of me. It was my duty to take over, eventually, the business my father had chosen. My dad operated a small trucking business, and my mother, a woman of energy and independence, had a business of her own, a small factory manufacturing Indonesian "batik" fabrics. But as a frail youngster, the very thought of having to boss a crew of burly, brawling truck drivers scared me and gave me bad dreams. Thoughts of taking the batik factory didn't scare me, they only bored me. "What an awful life that would be," I told myself. But what to do? It was my duty. One or the other. And I hated both options, so turned over and wept some more.

One morning when I was brooding and getting nowhere, it struck me that it might help to lock my door and go into a long period of Buddhist meditation. So I turned the key, loosened my collar, and took up the prescribed stance, cross-legged on the floor.

"Now, how do I start meditating?" I thought. I bowed my head and shut my eyes, but nothing came. So I sat up straight, tilted my head upward, and closed my eyes again. Still no powerful thoughts, just a mental blank. I was facing my bookshelves, and every time I opened my eyes with my head tilted upward, the first thing I saw was that little black Dutch New Testament.

"But, no," I told myself. "This is no time for reading, but for thinking. I must plan my life. I must think of Buddha, or at least, think of some way to spend my life that doesn't involve trucks and batik fabrics."

So I closed my eyes again and again. And every time I opened them, there was that little black book that I had never opened. After a while, I began thinking about the books on my shelf. From my position of meditation on the floor I looked at them, one at a time. Having read them all, I tried to recall what they said. This, I told myself, is a good way to start meditating. They are all good schoolbooks, so I will get some good thoughts. At least I'll be thinking about something, not just sitting here helplessly with a blank mind.

So I reviewed them, book by book. Having enjoyed them, I could give a good synopsis of every one. This seemed to go on for hours, although likely only a short time. Finally reaching the top shelf, only half way across it, I saw the little black book my friend had given me only a few days before, still unopened.

"What shall I do?" I asked myself. "This is a time for important meditation, and my life may be changed by my thoughts. So I'd better stick to my meditation. If I start reading now, I'll lose my train of thought." Then it occurred to me that I really hadn't developed any train of thought. I was just recalling the lessons contained in these old school books, which I knew by heart. The only one I couldn't review in my mind was that little black book. So I'd might as well read it, or at least look at a few pages. Then I could honestly say that I had read every book on all the shelves, and could give a good account of what was in them.

"It's such a small book," I noted mentally, "there can't be very much in it." So I unfolded my stiffened legs and arose painfully from the floor, rubbing the circulation back into the legs as I straightened them, and stretching my arms above my head to take the kinks out of my back. Then climbing onto a chair, I plucked the little gift volume from the top shelf and settled down again on the floor, my back propped against the bed, and opened it.

As if ordered by some mysterious power, the New Testament opened at the beginning of Paul's letter to the Romans. I began to read, with no real interest at first, and thought to myself that this Christian holy book seemed awfully dull. Finally I came to the passage in which Paul describes God's anger at the evil ways of people who prevent the truth from becoming known, and His anger at those who worship idols, and those who insist on worshiping the things that God had created, instead of worshiping the God who created them! This passage set my heart pounding faster. It was an idea, a concept of the relative importance of things that had never occurred to me. I began to feel twinges of conviction and guilt.

"This is exactly what I've been doing," I said aloud. "This is what we've all believed throughout our lives! Can we be wrong? I must read on and see what more this man has to say. Maybe this is the Almighty One speaking to me. Maybe my fears and my decision to meditate were all arranged by Him to lead me to this book. Anyway, these are certainly new thoughts to meditate. Now I am getting thoughts that may be worthwhile. I'll read some more. I can meditate later. Why had I never had such thoughts? Why did it never enter my mind that the wonders of nature could never be so great as the wonders of the God who created it all?"

This was an exciting new picture of the relationship of man to God. I could hardly wait to turn the little pages to find out what would come next. I read on where Paul describes the thought of these evil people as "nonsense" and pictures their minds as filled with emptiness and darkness.

"This book makes some sense!" I thought. My own mind, I recalled, had been filled with emptiness and darkness for several hours just passed. I had not had a new or constructive thought, but only recited things I had read and memorized in books. And not one of those books had been so excitingly new and mind-expanding as this one.

"But to accept this Jesus as my Lord and Savior? No way! He seems to have had some good ideas. But to give up my ancient Buddhist faith for this new foreign guru? No sir. It's going to take more than a few new ideas, even if they are interesting and important."

"But I will read more." So I settled down against my bed, with my legs stretched out on the floor, and went on reading.

Suddenly, it was as if I had been struck by a bolt of lightning! I came to the fifth chapter of Romans and what, to me, was an incredible revelation: "Now that we have been put right with God through faith, we have peace with God through our Lord Jesus Christ." I read, and my heart began to pound even harder with the excitement of the words, "He has brought us by faith into this experience of God's grace, in which we live. For when we were helpless, Christ died for the wicked, at a time that God chose."

"Peace with God!" I almost shouted. "That must be it! That is the answer. If I have peace with God, I don't have to be afraid of the future, or of the next life, or of anything else."

Behind my excitement – which may not be understandable to the Western mind long familiar with the teachings of Christ – was an Oriental conception of peace that is a lot like the idea the Jews express with the word "shalom." It denotes more than simply the cessation of war. It implies a complete peace, through the whole man – peace spiritually, physically, socially and mentally, and the experience of God's infinite grace in this life, and through eternity.

I threw my head back and leaned on the bed for a moment, thinking of the wonder of such a peace with God, the Supreme Being of the universe. Suddenly I felt an overwhelming compulsion to speak directly to this new God, to ask for mercy in the name of Jesus Christ, His Son, who according to this wonderful little book had come to earth to save all people, and had wiped out our sins by the sacrifice of His own life!

Then I heard myself say aloud: "Lord Jesus Christ, forgive me," I said. "I didn't know! I didn't know! I have been blind and ignorant. Forgive me!" Suddenly there was a feeling within me like an explosion. It was a surge of unutterable joy!

Then I became conscious of another presence in the room! It was as if hands had been placed on my head and shoulders. I turned and looked quickly around, fully expecting to see this new guru, this Jesus, right there in the room with me. No one was visible, but I knew deep within me that Jesus must have been there, for my feeling of extreme elation continued to grow.

Finally, I could restrain myself no longer! I jumped to my feet half-laughing, half-sobbing, and rushed out the door into the back yard as if the house were on fire.

Overcome by intense ecstasy, I ran through the yard embracing each tree, kissing each plant, and each flower, laughing and shouting as if I were drunk with joy, which I was. My feeling was one of overwhelming joy and adoration of the God who had opened such wonders to me in the Bible, His book. How clearly it was written! Nowhere in Buddhism or animism, with its thousands of gods – one behind every bush, so to speak – had I ever found any such direct and distinct statements, so clearly put, about the relationship of the Maker of the universe and the creatures that He had created.

If St. Francis of Assisi had been there in my back yard and seen me, he would have understood perfectly. He would have known immediately that I was praising the Lord by the effusive greeting of nature, and he would have been pleased, because he understood this kind of thing. But I have often wondered what my Buddhist friends would have thought, had any of them dropped by at that moment. They probably would have tackled me, thrown me to the ground, and called for the "men in the white jackets" to come and get me.

But for me it was a day of wonder! I suddenly felt that everything in the world was new. Even my outlook was new. The world had in a flash become a place of boundless wonder, instead of the pit of torment that I had pictured in my depression and brooding early in the day. What an extreme delight to be part of it all – and that it was all mine! Feeling so much joy, I began to weep. When the thought of my friends, and millions of other humans, not yet released from the fears and sorrows and worries of their man-made religions, I wept again. "I must tell them," I said aloud, "I must tell them."

"What awful mistakes we have been making," I thought. "And we have no excuse. For, as the Apostle Paul wrote in Romans: '...What can be known about God is plain to them, because God has shown it to them. Ever since the creation of the world His invisible nature, His eternal power and deity have been easy to perceive in the things that have been made. So they are without excuse. For although they knew God they did not honor Him as God, or give thanks to Him, but became futile in their thinking, and their senseless minds were darkened...(They) exchanged the glory of the immortal God for images resembling mortal man or birds or animals.'"

That passage hit me right between the eyes. For as animists, we had been worshiping old trees, birds, stones, reptiles, just about anything and everything, in fact, that God had created. But we had never turned our worship toward God, our creator.

Returning to the darkness of my room as the evening fell, I sat in the dark and pondered this enormous thing that had happened to me. The truth of Paul's letter to the Romans cut me like a knife, and left a throbbing sense of guilt. I had found the truth. I knew as a Buddhist that Gautama Buddha had never attempted to answer the mystery of death and what comes after it. But Jesus offered assurance of life beyond this world – a life of happiness and fulfillment, not a return trip to this world in the form of some lower animal. Jesus offered assurance of life beyond the present life because He conquered physical death. My Buddhist teachers had told me that I would have to wait through a long cycle of deaths and reincarnations before finding eternal peace. But Paul had brushed aside this "nonsense" showing that Christ had eliminated the need for punishment. By dying on the cross, He had removed our sins. Peace with God was available immediately. "What a wonderful truth to know!" "I must tell everyone."

Looking back now over the years that have passed since that day, I can see that the most important lesson in that whole glorious experience was the fact that I, a staunch pagan for 17 years, became a Christian by simply reading the New Testament in my locked room! The truth was clear, the words of the Apostle Paul convicted me of my error and my sins. I asked to be forgiven, accepted Christ by faith as my Savior, and was transformed from a brooding pagan into a joyful member of the body of Christ – all before I had ever spoken to another Christian. The Bible did its own missionary work.

I had a strange dream that changed the whole direction of my life only a few weeks after giving my life to Christ. One hot summer afternoon lying on my bed with my Bible beside my pillow, I must have dropped off to sleep. My experience was so real that I still am not sure whether I was sleeping and dreaming, or whether I saw a vision. Suddenly I saw a man come into the room. He was partly bald, and wearing a semi-saffron robe, somewhat like the robes the Buddhist monks wear.

Looking straight at me, he seemed to be pointing to something, some kind of book. I sat up quickly to get a closer look at the man and at the book, and to ask what he wanted in my room. The sudden movement must have awakened me, and when I looked around, the vision had vanished. There was no one else in the room.

It was all so vivid, so real that it left me trembling with excitement. I thought about the significance of that dream for a long time, and decided that the book was the Bible. I asked myself "Was it the Lord who caused this vision or dream?" The more I thought about it, the more convinced I became that it must have been a sign that God wanted me to devote my life to that Book. This was the beginning of my long road from paganism to the

Christian ministry. When my father, some time later, angrily protested my decision to attend a Christian college and study for the ministry, that vivid dream helped me stick to my decision. And every time I wavered in my resolve, when the burden of studies became heavy, the dream came back to remind me of what I believed to be a sign from God that He wanted me to work for Him.

From the very day of my conversion I have been a constant reader of the Bible.

In my first year as a Christian – my freshman year, so to speak – the New Testament was my whole Bible. I had only a vague knowledge that the Old Testament existed, but I devoured that little Dutch New Testament. In that first year, I read it through no less than a 100 times, committing long portions to memory. Every morning when the roosters began to crow about 4:00, I would sit in bed or on the floor and saturate myself with the Holy Scripture.

In these early months I was baffled by the unmerited love that God had bestowed on me. I wept a lot as I read. It puzzled me why such a large part of the human race was so callous and ungrateful for this divine love.

My father, who was still a Buddhist and Confucianist, worked himself up into a fury every time he caught me reading my Testament. Fearing he might have a heart attack in one of these tirades, I tried not to irritate him. He threatened to disown me, throw me out of the house, and thrash me. But I already was sufficiently schooled in the teachings of Jesus to know that a soft answer was called for. I knew that in his heart he loved me, and that he had no intention of carrying out his threats.

I became a fanatical Christian in my first year. A

little education is a dangerous thing. I had had only a little Christian education, and that came entirely from reading the New Testament, with no one to interpret or explain. More important, I had never read a word of the Old Testament.

So I was worried that my human weaknesses seemed to stay with me. I wanted to emerge from my conversion a full-blown saint. I punished myself cruelly for my shortcomings in that first year. This was likely a hangover from my years of Buddhist and Hindu teaching. I carved a crude crucifix for myself and knelt before it every night. I kept a written record of my failures and shortcomings – my sins – even of rebellious thoughts that entered my mind. As punishment for these things, I would force myself to take my bitter Atabrine tablets without the help of a glass of water or iced tea. I was still required to take these tablets to ward off attacks of malaria.

Sadly I was making the Christian life unpleasant. As a Buddhist I had been taught that suffering was a sign of devout faith. But nothing in the New Testament said I had to force sufferings on myself to prove that I was a Christian. Then, about a year after my conversion, I first got hold of a copy of the full Bible, including the Old Testament. This provided the missing link I needed to bring my newfound Christianity into true perspective.

For months I devoured the Old Testament as eagerly as I had the New Testament in my "freshman" year. It finally dawned on me that the great men of the Bible were not perfect. They all fell short of perfection. This lifted a great burden from me. I cannot recall ever afterward forcing myself to take a bitter pill without iced tea to blot out the taste. The Old Testament freed me to be patient, with a clear conscience, while waiting for the Lord to mold me into the kind of man He wanted me to be.

I read the story of Jeremiah, a man who ministered to kings in the name of the Lord. This holy man weakened to the point where he not only complained to God, but was so upset he even cursed his mother and father for bringing him into the world. He called on the Lord to destroy just about everyone who had come into his life! If Jeremiah could get away with that, I reasoned, then the Lord would not be too angry over my rebellious thoughts.

I admire the wisdom of God in the Psalms. One of my favorites in those early days was the picture in Psalm 1 of the godly man. He grows like a tree beside a stream of water, a tree that bears fruit in its season, not all the time, though its leaves remain green. I took comfort, also, in Paul's exhortation to be patient because our Christian growth only *starts* at the moment we accept Christ. He says in his second letter to the Corinthians that as we walk with the Lord we will be transformed by the Holy Spirit into the likeness of Jesus Christ Himself.

In my early Christian days I literally slept with my Bible. I underlined every new passage. In fact, I underlined so many that it became easier to find those that were not underlined. The most important thing I learned was to be patient. There is no such thing as an "instant Christian."

One of the most significant events of my early Christian life occurred in the late 1940s. It proves that God is still working the old-time biblical miracles among us today. This is what happened:

My maternal grandmother became seriously ill. Now at that time, as I recall, only my mother and I had accepted Christ. My grandfather was so bitterly anti-Christian that he vowed to burn every Bible that came into his house. It made him furious that my mother and I had "surrendered" to this "Jesus propaganda." At the same time he was an equally strong believer in Buddhism; he might have been described as a Buddhist zealot or radical. My grandmother was less radical, but solidly Buddhist.

Shortly after she became ill, the family was summoned to her bedside. She had lapsed into a coma, and it looked as if we were going to lose her. My grandfather, a well-known architect, was overcome with grief. The two were very close and extremely affectionate, to the end of their days.

Grandmother was in a coma for three days, unable to eat or drink. In those days intravenous feeding was unknown, so three days without food or water meant she was about to die. Mother and I prayed that the Lord would spare this gentle old lady. She was the mother who had shaped the character of my own beloved foster mother, and it seemed to me that if the Lord let her die, I could not stand the suffering it would cause my mother. But the rest of the family took a more realistic view. They bought a coffin, and contacted an undertaker to make plans for the funeral. As my grandmother neared death, one of my uncles, a son of my grandparents suggested somewhat fearfully that we call a Christian pastor to pray for my dear grandma – "if grandpa would permit it."

To our amazement, grandpa in his grief agreed. The doctor had declared her a hopeless case, so he undoubtedly felt this was no time for a squabble in the family.

So the local pastor was called. When he arrived at the bedside, he was greeted politely by grandpa and was told that he might "say whatever prayers you Christians say." The pastor, kneeling beside the bed, raised his face toward heaven and quietly asked the Lord, "if it be Thy will," to save this beloved lady and give her more years of life to enjoy with the family she has worked so hard to raise.

After his prayer, we sat in silence around the bed for a time. Then we began to notice, for the first time in days, a movement of her eyelids and the hands.

Thinking this must be the end, we drew near. As we did, my grandmother opened her eyes wide and struggled to sit up. Several of us reached out to help her. She looked around with a curious raising of her eyebrows, and asked us for a glass of milk. She said she was told to drink a glass of milk, which might do her some good.

With puzzlement all over our faces, we quickly complied with her request, and stood around watching as she drank the milk. Then she turned to the members of the family and asked, "Which one of you invited that delightful stranger to come to visit with me here?"

We looked at each other, not knowing what to say, thinking that poor "dying" grandma was a little out of her head. But she kept on asking about the stranger. And when we insisted that none of us had seen any stranger, she proceeded to tell us that we must have been blind, and she told this story:

"This gentleman was dressed in white. He wore a shiny robe, his face was so pleasant, that it seemed to radiate light like the sun, and he had the most beautiful long hair. He came right over here to my bed and told me, 'Please drink a glass of milk, and you will be well.' As he turned to go, he told me, 'Don't be afraid.'"

"You see, that's why I asked for a glass of milk, and now I must say I do feel much better."

42

From that moment on, grandma rapidly regained her strength. But the most radical change was in grandpa. He was firmly convinced that the Christian pastor had done the healing by calling on the Christian God to perform a miracle. He dropped his Buddhist faith on the spot, and became one of the most active Christians in the region. Grandma, too, and most of the other non-Christian members of the family came to Christ with him.

As the news of this miracle spread through the city, many who knew my grandfather and his bitter anti-Christian bias, were convinced that Christ was the true Savior and gave their hearts to Him. The story of my grandmother's healing is still being told in the churches there.

And, speaking of churches, my architect grandfather immediately went to the pastor who had prayed for grandma, and arranged for the construction of a new church building. Constructed in the late 1940s, that building still stands, and it is still filled with believers every Sunday. The faith of many of them dates back to grandmother's illness. Before he died, grandfather had designed and built a half dozen churches in Eastern Java, three of them in the main city, Surabaya.

The miracle of my grandmother's escape from death convinces me that real old-time Bible miracles are being used by the Lord to help bring unbelievers to Christ. The time is late, and I am sure that nothing short of miracles will bring them to abandon their ancient man-made religions. I often wonder if the same kind of miracles may be happening all around us here in America, and we perhaps are too sophisticated to accept them. ✝

Why The Angels Laughed

Chapter 5

Hopelessly In Love

I was hopelessly in love. I was in torment. To me, it really did seem hopeless. She was a smiling, friendly dark-eyed girl, with long, shiny black hair and a voice that sounded like the tinkling of silver bells. When she sang, I knew she must be an angel in disguise. And when she looked at me, I got chills and stammered.

I was certain she would not want to marry a skinny, spindle-legged Chinese like me. And I had good reason for my fears. Deborah – everyone called her Debbie – was Chinese, too. But there was an invisible wall between us. She was a different kind of Chinese. It was sort like the "Hatfields" and the "McCoys", only without the shooting.

In Indonesia, the Chinese community was sharply divided. There were the so-called "overseas-Chinese" – those who have lived abroad for generations and adopted the traditions and customs of their adopted land. Then there were the "Chinese-Chinese" – the families that have migrated from China in recent years, and still cling to their own Chinese dialect (there are many) and the customs and traditions of old China.

The two groups have always avoided social contacts. They spoke to each other only on business matters. Usually they had difficulty understanding each other because the overseas Chinese, especially the Dutch educated ones, abandoned the Chinese language generations ago. What was even worse, in my lovesick eyes, was the snobbery that grew up between the two groups. Do you see my impossible problem?

I was an overseas-Chinese, spoke Dutch and Indonesian, and had always been taught to look down on the Chinese-Chinese as social and intellectual inferiors.

Debbie was a Chinese-Chinese. She spoke beautiful Mandarin Chinese, and Indonesian when necessary. She had been brought up by strict parents, who warned her against having anything to do with those vulgar, mongrel, money-mad overseas-Chinese, who couldn't even speak their own language. Naturally, I assumed she was a dutiful daughter, and would obey her parents.

We were both students at a Christian college on the island of Java. My first ray of hope came when I learned that Debbie's father was a devout Buddhist-Confucianist, and that she had defied him and accepted Christ as her Savior. Even more significant, in my frantic, scheming mind, was the fact that she had stood up to her non-Christian father again in choosing a college. He gave in finally, and allowed her to attend this Christian school.

I could sympathize with the plight of Debbie's father. How could any father be angry at this lovely girl, or refuse her anything she wanted? I "worshiped" her.

All my hopes hinged on the vital fact that we were both Christians. That, I hoped, would reduce the height of that impassable wall between us. Maybe.

So I continued to "worship" from a distance for a time, doing my best to concoct plots that would make it necessary for me to speak to her. I had not counted on a miracle to bring us together, but God had planned a miracle just ahead. If I had known this, I would have been saved much lovesick misery.

The miracle came about like this. Our school was Chinese-oriented, and much of the class work was in Chinese, some in English, and some in Indonesian. So when the school authorities found that I, an overseas-Chinese, had no knowledge of any Chinese dialect, they decided that I should have a Chinese language tutor, and take an intensive course so I could keep up with my studies.

That was when the miracle happened! There was a knock on my door the afternoon after I had been told that they would send me a tutor. I opened it, and there stood Debbie – my own lovely Debbie – smiling shyly at me and holding a Chinese-language Bible under her arm! It was Debbie the school authorities had picked to teach me Mandarin Chinese!

I was so overcome that I didn't even hear what she said to me, at first. When I didn't reply, she repeated again that she had been sent to teach me Chinese. Still we stood in the doorway. Finally, I regained my senses and invited her to come in, but still could not believe what was happening. It must be a dream! It certainly was a miracle, an answer to my secret prayers!

Debbie was very prim and businesslike. She announced that she had brought the Chinese Bible along because she had been told that I was familiar with the Bible in Dutch and Indonesian. So it had occurred to her that the Bible in Chinese would be the very best kind of a textbook for me.

I agreed eagerly. But, of course, I would have agreed with anything she said at that moment, so anxious was I not to disrupt this wonderful thing that had happened. And we started that afternoon with the first of my lessons in Mandarin Chinese.

It had never occurred to me that Debbie Giam – Giam was the family name – might be very intelligent, as well as the most beautiful and desirable girl in all of Indonesia, if not the whole world. That first day I sat there in a sort of trance. Every time she looked down to read from her Chinese Bible, I would stare at her, drinking in every detail, from her beautiful hair to her dainty feet. When she looked up I would quickly shift my gaze back to the Bible in my own lap, and then fail completely to follow her in the proper Mandarin pronunciation. I could see that my lovely teacher was not too happy with my progress that first day, and that frightened me. I banished the thought that she might give up in disgust, and ask the school people to send someone else in her place. So I resolved to control my emotions the next time, and show her that, even though I was one of the overseas-Chinese that her people looked down upon, I wasn't dumb.

So now, wonder of wonders, I had a legitimate excuse to be with Debbie every day! And I did my best to make skinny Eddy Swieson look and act like a man she might consider as a husband.

Part of my plan was to study the Mandarin Chinese language as I had never studied before, and in this way impress her that I was smart, if not the handsomest man on the campus. So that's the way I studied, early and late, and always waited eagerly for her arrival the next day.

Soon I noticed that my teacher had begun to relax, and was less shy. We engaged more frequently in small talk about things apart from Mandarin Chinese. As I was learning a lot about the Chinese language, Debbie was quite frank in her comments to me. She said she was very happy with the way I was learning. And I, of course, was profuse in my praise of her talents as a teacher!

After three months, I was able to read many passages from the Chinese Bible quite well. Debbie had abandoned her shyness, and would actually clap her hands in applause when I finished a particularly difficult passage with minimum errors. I noted this secretly in my heart, and told myself, "You're making good progress, Eddy." I did not mean progress in my studies!

After six months I understood most of the lectures of the Chinese professors, even the most intellectual of them.

After only nine months of study with Debbie, there came a wonderful day when the dean of students asked Debbie how I was doing. On the basis of her report, the dean asked me to serve as an interpreter from Chinese into Indonesian for some of the Chinese instructors! I remember that day particularly, not because of the honor of being asked to interpret, but because I used the excitement of the moment, and took advantage of the obvious look of pleasure in the eyes of the beautiful Debbie, to do something I had never dared do before. I took her in my arms and held her close for a moment, my cheek against hers, and whispered my thanks into her ear. She pulled away quickly and gave me an embarrassed smile. But my heart leaped with joy! "I think she likes me!" So I quickly told her that we must continue with the lessons.

"I want to learn Mandarin Chinese well enough to preach a sermon in it," I told her. "You must continue to help me." She smiled in a way that I thought was a happy smile, and said she would continue. Then she added, "The school said I should teach you for one year, and we have been studying together for only nine months." Again I felt a pang of fear. Was she doing this because the school asked her to or because I did? I would have to intensify my campaign of conquest. I vowed silently that when I preached my first sermon in Mandarin Chinese, Debbie Giam would be sitting in the chapel to share my accomplishment as my proud bride-to-be, not simply as the teacher who made the sermon in Chinese possible.

That's the way it happened. Those last three months of study with Debbie strayed away from strictly Bible study, and wandered frequently into conversational Chinese and some very personal subjects, like the beauty of her complexion, the shine of her hair. Then we began to talk of our plans – our individual plans – for the future. We found that we both had a call to spread the Gospel. I told her that a wonderful singing voice like hers would be a tremendous help in Christian crusades. In that way, we knew that God had meant us for each other. The formal words of proposal seemed superfluous when I finally summoned up the nerve to say them out loud to Debbie, as I had practiced them so many times before my mirror.

We were gloriously happy together for about one day. Then we faced the sobering fact that her Buddhist father, who literally hated the Christian religion, and my newly Christian parents, who still clung to the ancient Chinese tradition that the parents do the matchmaking, had never been told what was going on.

50

How to break it to them? My mother, like a lot of other mothers who have only one son, was always jealous of my girl friends, and inclined to be sharply critical of them. She was furious when I switched girl friends without consulting her. And she never failed to disagree with my choice. Although I loved her dearly, I was still a little afraid of her. She had always been such a stern disciplinarian. But I felt that she was seldom right in her criticism of my girl friends.

The one she disliked most of all was the girl I was keeping company with, when I first caught sight of Debbie. I had told my mother that I was thinking seriously of asking her to be my wife. Well, my mother let go with such a tirade against this girl that it shocked me. She was really a fine girl and beautiful, and came from a good family. Many years later, my mother knew she was wrong in that instance, because the young woman became a Christian missionary in West Irian, the Indonesian half of New Guinea.

Debbie had already overruled her father concerning her choice of the Christian religion, and her choice of a Christian college. So we felt it could be done again, in the matter of a husband. But my mother had us scared. We didn't want to launch our married life with a family battle. So we spent hours planning how we would break the news to my foster mother, Rini Tan, and to my father. They were both staunch members of the "Hatfield-McCoy" feud with the Chinese-Chinese faction. They were disdainful of these relatively new arrivals in Indonesia (Debbie's father migrated from Fukien Province when he was 14 years old. But that looked like a short time ago to my parents, who were both born to families that had lived in the former Dutch East Indies for a couple of generations.)

51

Even while we worried about breaking the news of our love for each other, the Lord stepped in with another miracle to help our romance along. It didn't look much like a miracle at first, because it started when I got sick. There was persistent pain in my stomach that would not go away. It got so bad, finally, that my mother and father rushed over to the college to see me. And the minute my mother saw me she ordered me to a hospital where I was examined by a surgeon.

Not a moment too soon! The doctor discovered that I was suffering from an attack of appendicitis, and I was rushed to the operating room. My appendix, which was about to burst, was removed, and I was bedded down in a hospital room to recuperate. For the next day or so I had time to think, and I devised what seemed like a desperate, but workable, plot.

I wasn't afraid to tell my father, because Debbie's beauty and charm would be enough to convince him. But mother was something else. I began to think along these lines: Here am I, poor, sick Eddy, lying in a hospital. Surely if I tell my mother about Debbie now in the presence of some of my visiting friends, she will restrain herself from any snap judgment against my bride-to-be.

So I asked my parents to summon one of my former girl friends, one of whom they had not voiced too strong an objection, and they called her to come over. When I got a chance to whisper to her for a moment, I told her my problem and begged her to act as "go-between" to ease the news to my parents.

Reluctantly, she agreed "but only because you are sick." She added, "This probably isn't going to work, so don't blame me. It was your own idea."

So it was arranged that the next day my former girl friend, Mary, would bring Debbie to the hospital

with her when she came to visit me. And, while Debbie
was in the room, Mary was to whisper to my mother to
go out in the hall, and there my mother was to be told
that "Eddy wants to marry this lovely Chinese girl who
is such a good Christian and has such a lovely voice,
and would make such a good wife for a young Christian
minister when he starts preaching and holding
meetings." With all that endorsement, I thought, my
mother will have a hard time finding reasons to say no.

Well, at first, everything went as planned. Debbie
arrived with my former girl friend, and greeted me very
formally and sympathetically. Then Mary whispered to
my mother, and the two of them went out into the
hospital hallway.

I immediately grabbed Debbie by the hand and
whispered, "Pray!" We both closed our eyes and prayed
silently that the Lord would bless this venture. My
father must have suspected that something was up,
when he saw me holding Debbie's hand. But we said
nothing. It seemed like hours before my mother and my
friend came back into the room.

There was no telltale expression on my mother's
face. Then Mary gave me a wink and a quick nod that
seemed to signal everything was okay. Nothing more
was said. Mary's wink gave me a lift, and I began to
chatter happily. My mother finally remarked that they
had all better leave before I tired myself talking too
much.

As Debbie turned to go, I caught her eye and gave
her the "okay" nod and a big smile. She winked when no
one was looking, but maintained the appearance of a
circumspect young Chinese lady who was not yet aware
that a "go-between" had just settled the arrangements
for our marriage.

Later that day, when mother returned to the hospital alone, we talked about Debbie and our plans. With some show of face-saving hesitation she said Debbie might turn out to be a reasonably good choice for me, adding that she had been thinking that it was about time for me to take a wife. "People don't like their ministers to be single men," she explained. "It causes talk in the church and can cause trouble."

Both families put up a good show of forgetting to "look down" on each other at our wedding. It was a happy affair, and a pleasant memory. We were married on June 25, 1957, only a few days after we graduated from college. This was Debbie's birthday. ✟

Chapter 6

Praying with Thanksgiving

It was my deep conviction that God wanted me to be in the ministry of sharing the Good News of God's salvation. He implanted in my heart a passion for people whom I met to experience the joy of life, which our Risen Savior alone could impart. So, after Debbie and I graduated from college in June 1957 and were married a few days later, I began to look for a good theological school. But where? And how? The best nearby were in Australia. But even "nearby" in the South Pacific was a long way, almost 4000 miles. But there were even more serious obstacles than distance. We found that we were virtually prisoners in Indonesia.

Governmental mismanagement under the Sukarno revolutionists had brought the country to the point of bankruptcy. Rigid controls on foreign exchange blocked all travel abroad by Indonesians, except in the most extreme urgency. Even travel between the islands was controlled. Permits were required for imports and exports. Communications were restricted. As members of the small Chinese minority, we were suspected of both Dutch and Communist leanings, with no chance of any special favors from the Sukarno regime.

It looked hopeless. But we were young, optimistic, very much in love, and most important, sure the Lord wanted us to work for Him, so we knew He would find a way. We knelt in our temporary rooms, near my parents' home, and told the Lord our troubles. Even if our parents were willing to pay our fare to Australia, the exchange controls blocked them. And there was still the school tuition and living costs to consider. Also, there was the important matter of being admitted to the school of our choice, since Australia was enforcing a strict quota on non-white immigrants and students.

While we waited and prayed, we wrote to some of our Australian friends for information about the colleges and the costs, and also told them of our financial needs. The people we considered friends were mostly pastors and missionaries I had helped as an interpreter while in college. We felt the closest to the Reverend Reginald Wright, a Baptist pastor in Perth, and Dr. Harold Steward, a surgeon who had worked in Christian hospitals in Java between 1955 and 1957.

Within six weeks – about the length of time it took for the mail to make the round trip – both our prayers and our letters were answered. Reginald Wright had talked to the authorities of Adelaide Bible Institute in South Australia, and that school granted me a scholarship to study for the Melbourne College of Divinity, Licentiate in Theology.

Now, under the Australian system, divinity courses from the prestigious Melbourne College of Divinity could be taken at other authorized schools, including the school to which I now had a scholarship. I was elated. But then a new thought struck me. I couldn't leave Debbie behind, didn't even have the money to make the trip myself. We were sure that the Lord didn't want to separate us, after bringing us together.

So we continued our prayers. A few days later, as I was walking near our home, the postman came by and handed me a letter with an Australian postmark. With trembling hands I tore open the envelope. It was from Dr. Steward. Folded into the letter was the official student permit for Debbie. The Stewards had voluntarily sponsored Debbie, when they learned that Reginald Wright was sponsoring me! I ran the half-mile home and threw my arms around Debbie. We knelt again, thanking our Lord for His kindness to us.

The way was opening, there was a scholarship waiting in Adelaide, and we were both cleared to enter the country and stay until I earned my L.Th. But still, there was no money to make the trip. For weeks we prayed and waited daily that this last barrier would be lifted. Our parents agonized with us. My father, who had sold his trucks, had a bank account full of Indonesian rupiahs, but they were useless for foreign travel.

As we were praying one day, it came to me that we were not giving any evidence of our confidence in God's goodness and care. So I said to Debbie, "Let's stop praying for now, and go down to the Australian consulate and start cutting through the red tape to get our visas. The Lord has done very well so far. I know He's going to finish the job."

So that's what we did. It took the usual hours of waiting in bureaucratic offices. But we had the needed documents, and finally got our visas. Back home, we knelt again to thank God for giving us full clearance for the trip. Then I thought we were again being a little weak in our faith. So we stopped praying and asking, rose to our feet, and started praising the Lord for solving all of our problems.

As we sang together, we thought we heard a knock on the door. So we stopped for a moment, and the knock came again. Standing outside was one of our former instructors from Sydney, Australia with an envelope in her hand. With a big smile she said to us, "Folks, I am pleased to hand you two airlines tickets for you to fly to Australia." The Lord kept on providing all our needs to study in Australia.

When we arrived in Adelaide, I ran into an unexpected problem. The seasons are reversed in Australia from what they are here in the United States and in Southeast Asia. Summer comes in our winter months, and winter in our summer. So the school year there begins in February and ends in November. And as school year ends, the nationwide uniform examinations are given, and they get wide publicity in newspapers.

We had arrived in August, after graduating in June. I had signed up for three courses, all of them in English, which was a fairly new language for me. And the final examinations in these courses – which had started the previous February – were due within three months of the time I signed in. Some friends advised me to skip the exams and repeat the courses the next school year, beginning in February.

But I was afraid my student permit might run out before I could complete my studies. So I put myself on an eighteen-hours-a-day study schedule. Sympathetic fellow students filled me in on parts that I had missed. I read and reread books that had been used as texts. Debbie studied beside me, and helped by questioning me, to make sure I understood.

On the eve of the examination, at the Wesley Theological Seminary in Adelaide in November 1957, we knelt and asked the Lord whether He really wanted me to try the exam. A failure could endanger my scholarship. But after three months of cramming, I believed the Lord would clear my mind and help me get at least a passing grade.

So I took the exam. In the weeks of waiting, I was nervous, despite all that the Lord had done in the past. Then, in December, the Adelaide newspapers published the names of local students who had passed the national examinations. Eagerly, we ran down the column of names. "Isn't it there? It should be right here in the 'E' section," I said, as my heart leaped in alarm. I felt a heavy sinking in my stomach, and tears of disappointment began to rise. Then I heard Debbie shriek in excitement. "Here is it," she cried. "Here it is! They've got you listed in the 'I' section, right here. Look 'Ie Eddy'" This was the first of a long series of incidents that finally convinced me to Anglicize my Chinese name.

I got a lot more than schooling out of my stay in Australia, having many opportunities for preaching and making speeches. As one of the few Asians in the school, I was a curiosity. Churches invited me to share the story of my conversion, and tell of Christian activity in Indonesia. I was invited to speak to conventions and rallies. I came to know many of the church leaders in Australia, who gave me invaluable advice. My speaking and preaching also helped to pay our expenses and improve my English. I was then a member of the Dutch Reformed Church in Indonesia, which after the revolution had separated from the Dutch Church, but retained brotherly ties and the same evangelical doctrines. Both were members of the World Presbyterian Alliance.

But my Christian friends and my speaking activities were not confined to this denomination. For example, I had many friends among the Methodists in Adelaide. Knowing of my financial stress, they

convinced the South Australia Methodist Conference
that it would be a fine Christian act to lend me a helping
hand.

Besides, they argued, "Eddy has a fine Christian
witness," and having a Chinese preacher would help
convince the world that Australians are not the racial
bigots that their immigration laws make them appear to
be.

So the Methodist Conference voted to make me a
temporary local preacher in the Adelaide Payneham
Circuit. Everywhere I was received with openhearted
Christian kindness. Hopefully my experience helped to
ease the immigration restrictions a few years later.

Finally, my three wonderful years in Australia
came to an end with God's immeasurable blessing! I had
my Licentiate in Theology and a burning desire to set
the East Indies, if not the whole world, on fire for Christ.
But first we had to make the trip home. We had never
traveled by ship, so this seemed like a wonderful
opportunity to have that experience, and also a pleasant
two weeks of rest aboard ship. As usual, I could not
envision complete rest, so I brought along my Greek
New Testament, thinking I could get through it before
the end of the voyage.

We brushed aside warnings about the possible
effects of sea travel as first-time ocean passengers, and
planned only for fun and reading. We sailed out of
Sydney harbor on the beautiful new Italian ship,
Neptunia, breathing the salt air deeply and enjoying the
unbelievable beauty of the scene. But no sooner had we
passed under the famous Sydney Bridge than the ship
began to roll and I became deathly seasick.

Eating proved to be impossible. For several days
all I could do was stay in my cabin, flat on my back. I
didn't even glance in the direction of that Greek New
Testament. I expected to die before we reached land.

And as the malady clung on, I remembered with sympathy the story of seasickness an Australian friend had told me. He had said that just before the end of his sickness his fear was not that he would die, but that he would not die. That gave me hope. He had survived and said that he even enjoyed the final days of his voyage.

Just as my friend predicted, I soon began to feel better. First, I sat up and drank some clear soup. Then I ventured on deck to breathe in the fresh sea air, and finally got up the nerve to scramble up the steep stairs to the very top deck. There I stood for a while, breathing in the healing air and looking at the sky and clouds, and the sea birds that dived and swooped around us. Everything looked clean and fresh and beautiful, especially this lovely ship. The sky was like a blue canopy over the dark green sea. Schools of flying fish were skimming now and then beside us. The beauty of this quiet scene made me forget, for a time, the still uncertain feeling in my stomach.

Drinking in this scene and clinging to the ship's rail, my thoughts moved on from the visible to the invisible, to the great God of the universe, the Maker of all this beauty. The first chapter of Genesis seemed to pass before me, as in a movie. My heart surged up and overflowed with deep emotion. I began to sing aloud, and to praise the Lord in a voice that was almost a shout, but was carried away by the wind. I stayed in that glorious spot for what seemed like hours, communing with the Lord of all creation. At times I wept, being constrained by the infinite love of my heavenly Father!

The next morning I returned to the same place, and again had the feeling of semi-detachment from earthly things. I praised God aloud and in my heart for His wonderful creation. Every day from that time until we reached Jakarta harbor, I made the top deck my place of morning prayer and praise.

This turned out to be a significant experience in my life, not just a passing moment. These days of joy and prayer on the top deck of the Neptunia revolutionized my praying. Up to this time, I had always thought the only way to pray was to go into a room, lock the door, get on my knees, close my eyes, and go through a list of requests to the Lord. But now I could talk to God in the open air with my eyes open, even while standing or walking. This new, unconventional way of praying gave me such joy that it became a part of my lifelong routine. It has stayed with me to this day.

Now, whether I am walking down the street, working in my yard, sitting in a park, or driving an automobile, I can talk to God and think of His promises and His presence. Often in these mobile talks with my heavenly Father, I am so moved that tears run down my face, and I speak aloud, though there is no one but the Lord to hear me.

Occasionally the thought comes to me that I might never have found this wonderful way of communion with my Maker, if I had not suffered through that agonizing sea trip. I firmly believe that there is value, spiritual value in suffering. My suffering on that trip led me to the secret of a way to toss aside the pressures and cares of everyday life, as if they didn't exist.

It seemed that everything had changed in the three years that we were away from Indonesia. After our three years in Australia, a country suffering (or possibly enjoying) under-population, what struck me hardest were the masses of people everywhere in Indonesia. I could appreciate what I learned in school: that Java, with 75 million people crowded into an area about the size of New York State, was the most heavily-populated spot on earth. And I noted that among these crowds of adults there were thousands upon thousands of children, testifying to the certainty that the future in Java is likely to be more crowded than the past.

The military seemed to be everywhere. Soldiers were in buses, in buildings, on the streets. Revolt had been spreading among the outer islands against the Sukarno regime, which held the island of Java. At the same time, the conflict between the revolutionaries and the Dutch was continuing.

I was saddened to find that many of my Dutch friends were gone. Most of them, in fact. All persons of Dutch ancestry had been ordered to return to the Netherlands, or to go somewhere else. To this Dutch-oriented Chinese, it hardly seemed like home, with so many friendly Dutch faces gone.

About a year before our return, Sukarno had scrapped his revolutionary constitution and reenacted the 1945 constitution which made the country virtually a dictatorship. Just before we landed, the new dictator dissolved parliament. He began to rule by executive decree, and took away all economic privileges of Dutch citizens. The communist-oriented dictator also abrogated his promise to pay for the nationalized properties taken away from their Dutch owners. This amounted to about one billion dollars. Chinese citizens, suspected by Sukarno of pro-Dutch sympathies, also suffered property seizures and the humiliation of being ordered to discard their Chinese names and assume new names in line with Indonesian names.

So it was a tense and unhappy country that we returned to. The very day of our arrival a lone rebel fighter plane from one of the rebellious outer islands made a sweep over the presidential palace, and fired machine guns and rockets into the building. We were riding in a bus when this happened, and were forced to get out of the vehicle and take shelter for about an hour.

It seemed, on the whole, a poor time to try to bring the teachings of Jesus Christ, the Prince of Peace, to my unhappy friends and neighbors. They were living in a virtual state of war. But God had called us, and Debbie and I were determined to plunge into our new work.

I was invited to teach in a Christian college, with the proviso that I would spend my weekends working among the young people of the Indonesian Christian Church (formerly the Dutch Reformed Church) in Malang where the college was located. I accepted immediately. So we settled down in that lovely town on the island of Java. Later, with the consent of the church session, Debbie was employed to help with the music and the singing.

It became a lively, active congregation. So many university students and young professionals joined, that after we started our youth work, we began a 7:00 A.M. service on Sundays. The regular service remained at 10:00 A.M. Within a year, the early service became so popular that the sanctuary simply could not accommodate the hundreds of people who came.

Then we launched a Thursday afternoon Bible study mainly for the young. As interest rose, we scheduled a daily prayer session, starting from 5:30 – 6:30 in the morning – timed so that students and workers could get to their regular daily routine. (In the Asian tropics working hours normally run from 7:00 A.M. to noon. After two hours of siesta time, work continues from 2:00 to 5:00 P.M.).

From this prayer meeting a Bible study group gradually formed. It met every Thursday in the church for serious discussion of the problems of Christians and their responsibility in their homes, schools and offices.

The eager interest in these discussions convinced me to give more attention to interpreting the Scriptures, and how they apply to everyday living. Putting the Bible on a practical level, I believe, makes Christianity more attractive, especially to those who daily face down-to-earth problems.

After a year of this kind of work, spreading my time between the college and the church, I was asked to be a full-time youth worker. The session (the body of ruling officers of the Reformed church) at the same time asked me to drop the work at the college and become a full-time member of the church staff. Up to this time I had been a sort of apprentice. So I had reached an important goal. And on my 29th birthday, November 28, 1961, I was ordained and installed as a minister of the Indonesian Reformed Church.

My mother came to Christ shortly before I did, but my father took more convincing. He denounced us both for abandoning our ancient faith Buddhism. There were angry scenes and violence, when mother announced her firm determination to support me in my decision to abandon the family business as a career and enter the ministry. My father angrily branded me as a thankless son for rejecting the trucking business that he had created. Things were in quite a mess at home when, suddenly, my father, who had seemed well, suffered a heart attack and was rushed to the hospital.

For a time, it looked like he was going to die. Mother and I, ignoring what we knew of his dislike for Christianity, knelt by his bed and prayed the Lord would restore him to us. A visiting minister from Hong Kong, the late Dr. Timothy Dzao, prayed with us. We urged my father to ask the Lord to forgive him his sins and bring him back to health.

With death staring him in the face, he finally began to weep. His obstinate spirit broke, and he prayed. The next day returning to the hospital, we were astounded at his improved appearance. A few days later the hospital said he was ready to go home.

Within weeks he was as robust and active as ever. On the day he left the hospital, he was carrying a Chinese Bible under his arm. He had been studying the Book of Ecclesiastes, which he said seemed familiar to him, because it was so similar to the teachings of Confucius.

My father was genuinely converted to Christ, and was so grateful for the restoration of his health that he decided to enter the Christian ministry. He sold his trucking business and returned to school. There it became obvious that he did not have a great future as a minister, but it was discovered that he had a great gift for learning and speaking foreign languages. So he studied to become an interpreter for visiting speakers and missionaries in Java.

He lived for 10 years after that heart attack, and became one of the most popular and most sought-after interpreters in Indonesia. His reputation for interpreting sermons from English to Indonesian or from Chinese to Indonesian was spread far beyond the borders of Indonesia by the visiting ministers of the Gospel. ✞

Chapter 7

Triumphal Harvest for the Lord

The rain came down like a thundering waterfall! Roads were flooded and impassable. Streams and rivers overflowed. The water rose to bridge level, and then began to flow across the tops of bridges. Nobody could remember any rain like it. Such a cloudburst! Such a torrential downpour! And still it came down, hour after hour.

To me, an eager young minister assigned to my very first efforts as an evangelist for the Reformed Church, it looked like the work of the Devil. As I looked out the window at the rising flood that first morning in Tasikmalaya, the West Java town where I was beginning a series of five evangelistic meetings that very evening, I felt a wave of bitter disappointment sweep over me. "Defeated," I thought. "Defeated by the Devil, even

67

before I get a chance to start my ministry."

Debbie was with me as we met with the church officers to discuss the situation, and decide whether or to cancel the service for that night. We agreed that it would be futile to expect people to come to church when most of them were trying furiously to protect their homes and property against damage from flooding. So we swallowed our disappointment and knelt together and asked God politely, that if He had the time and it was His will, we would appreciate it if He would stop this awful rain, if not today, then maybe in time for tomorrow's meeting. It was a childish sort of prayer. We were really saying, "After all, Lord, we are here to do your work and it seems the least you can do is give us decent weather."

We rose from our knees with heavy hearts, the rain still drumming on the roof. But we had second thoughts about canceling. The services had been widely advertised, and if even a few came out, in spite of the terrible weather, the least we could do was have the church open, and stand ready to go ahead with the preaching service. Besides, we thought, a little bit of hymn singing, and a song or two from Debbie, might help to lift our spirits. So we went ahead with preparations.

I was deeply engrossed with my sermon, and with Bible reading, when I began to sense a change. It was about 3:00 in the afternoon, and for a moment, as I struggled to shift my mind from my studies to what was going on around me, I couldn't place what distracted me. Then it struck me! The rain had stopped! At least, I couldn't hear it any more! I walked quickly to the window. It was true! No more rain! Not a drop was falling! The clouds were breaking up, and the sun was beginning to send needles of light across the soggy landscape.

Water on the streets was flowing off rapidly. The Lord had heard our child-like prayers and stopped the storm! So we knelt again with joy leaping in our hearts and gave thanks and praise to our all-powerful Creator.

The word spread quickly through the city. "It was a miracle," they were saying. "The pastor and the evangelist prayed, and the rains stopped. How lucky we are that the Christian meeting was tonight! We might have been flooded out of our homes. This is a mysterious thing. But it has happened before our eyes."

The service was to start at 6:00. By 5:00 the sanctuary was filled to capacity, and still they came. At 5:30, when we came to the church, we had to push our way through the crowd on the parking lot and in the streets. Inside the sanctuary, even the aisles were packed. Someone had called the police to clear the streets for traffic. Amplifiers were produced from somewhere, so the people outside could hear. There were overflow crowds and bright skies, and that's the way it went for five full days.

The meeting was the talk of the town. How wonderful of God to stop that unnatural downpour and transform the climate for a week so His messenger could bring the Gospel to the people of Tasikmalaya. What I had mistakenly thought was a work of the Devil, turned out to be the beginning of a miracle that brought thousands of non-believers to the meetings, many of whom accepted Jesus as their Savior.

The miracle of the stopping of the rain in Taskimalaya transformed the first crusade of an unknown evangelist into a triumphal harvest for the Lord, throughout the two months we were on the road. I had been assigned to this 1961 effort by the East Java Synod, which had appointed me to the Committee for Evangelism soon after my ordination. The area assigned to me covered the three provinces of East, Central and West Java.

There was another happening during this first crusade that might be classified as a miracle. We traveled by train, and at one point passed through a jungle region where rebels had been attacking trains by planting homemade explosive devices to derail them. Then they would move in to rob, and sometimes kill certain passengers.

Shortly before we passed that way, a train had been sabotaged, and several passengers died in the battle between the rebels and the troops that always rode the trains as guards.

We peered out the windows of the coach nervously, as our train moved into the dangerous zone. Troops aboard our car stood on the platforms at each entrance door, with rifles cocked and ready. Windows were ordered tightly closed, despite the heat and the humidity, and the atmosphere inside the cars grew stuffy and sickening.

The train crept on at what seemed like an unnecessarily low speed, and we unconsciously moved our bodies to try to make it go a little faster. Then there was a screeching, scraping sound, and the train jerked to a halt. We waited breathlessly, expecting shouts and gunfire. A trainman came running through the cars, and called over his shoulders as he ran that it was "nothing." He said there was "trouble with the brakes. We will be going in a moment."

But there we sat for nearly an hour. A stalled train, filled to capacity with passengers, was an invitation to rebels for robbery. There was not a movement, not a sound from the trees that bordered the tracks so closely on either side. Finally, to our great relief, there was a shrill whistle from the locomotive, and we began to move again. We said a silent prayer of thanksgiving.

Only a few days later we read in the newspapers that another train had been derailed in that same dangerous region, killing scores of passengers. All had been robbed of their possessions. Surely, the Spirit of God had protected us, as we sat there in a train that was disabled, and could not have escaped.

The second series of meetings in my "rookie" tour as an evangelist in 1961 was held in a big Methodist church in Jakarta, a city of sophisticated university students, government officials, and professionals. In my heart I was concerned that these educated people would soon see through my thin veil of theological learning, and would leave me with many empty seats after their first experience under my preaching.

In my anxiety to do my best to be eloquent and persuasive, I forgot the great truth that the messengers of God must always keep in mind: It is the Holy Spirit working with you, who brings people to Christ. You may stutter and stumble, and feel you have failed. But if the Spirit of God is with you, you cannot fail.

The story of the stopping of the rain had arrived ahead of me, and the large Methodist sanctuary was packed the first night. After the meeting I thought, "They've heard my simple sermon now. There'll be plenty of empty seats tomorrow." But the second night every seat was filled, and there was little standing room left! For the final three nights the city fathers sent police to keep the streets clear and traffic moving through the crowds that listened to the services standing outside the church.

Our performance was never altered. I had prepared only five sermons, one for each night at each city. Debbie sang, our musicians played, and there were prayers and announcements until everyone was assembled. And then I preached. The response always overwhelmed me. I know now that the thousands who made commitments to Christ in those meetings could not have been so convicted merely by the simple sermons of my beginning years. The Holy Spirit was at work in Indonesia, and Eddy was only "fronting" for Him.

Forewarned by the unexpected enthusiasm in our first two cities, we took the precaution of warning the police in advance when we reached Semarang, in Central Java. We told them we expected a large crowd, and asked for "an officer" to keep order.

The officers were polite, but it was obvious they didn't think there would be enough interest in a Christian revival in that city to warrant police help. They said they would surely come if needed, leaving the clear impression they were going to forget it. But by the second night, after a traffic snarl caused by our crowds the first night, the police turned out in force.

In the city of Solo, the sophisticated cultural center of Central Java, and again in the overwhelming Muslim city of Bondowoso there was evidence the Spirit of God was moving. Hundreds of Muslims accepted Christ, and on the last night the local Christians and many of the new converts begged us to continue the meetings there. "The revival has only begun here," they said. "Stay with us and we can win this whole province for Christ!" But we were set and advertised and ready to start the following week in Surabaya, the capital city of East Java. So we reluctantly and tearfully closed our final prolonged meeting with song and praise and prayers of thankfulness. Then we packed and moved on.

Surabaya was the city where I went to high school. We will never forget that experience! It was a fitting climax to an unexpectedly glorious crusade. Our meetings were to be held in the biggest Reformed church in the capital city. But several hours before the starting time the church officers came to me in breathless amazement.

"The sanctuary is filled already!" they reported. "And now people are gathering in the parking lots. They have brought chairs and pillows to sit on. We must find larger quarters. Do you mind if we rent the municipal auditorium? The police and the fire inspectors are complaining already that the church is over-full."

It was too late to change locations the first night, and we sang and preached to a packed sanctuary and to many hundreds outside by amplifiers. The second night even the bigger municipal auditorium was filled and hundreds more listened outside. This was heady stuff for a young preacher. Debbie was always there to dampen my ego, when I made some remark that hinted I was beginning to take the credit for all this excitement.

She would ask with a sly smile, "Was it you who stopped the rain at Tasikmalaya?" That was enough. I got the message.

The Surabaya police, incidentally, were getting a little irritable by the time our meeting closed. If ours had been an Islamic gathering they would have controlled the crowds without comment. That's because 95% percent of the populace were Muslim, and so were the police. But there was nothing in the book of police regulations that called for assisting at meetings of Christians. There weren't supposed to be enough Christians in the city to disrupt traffic. That is why we were so excited. We knew that the majority of those who came to our meetings must be non-believers, because there were hardly that many members in all the Christian churches combined. When the final meeting ended, the people were reluctant to leave. The local pastors begged us to continue, but we could not.

Before we left for home, the local pastors made one more effort to continue the meetings beyond the five days. They told us they could get the Surabaya stadium for a week, if we would stay. It was the ultimate compliment, and I prayed about it. But, all along, I knew in my heart that it was best to "stop while we were ahead," as the gamblers say. I had preached all of my five sermons!

A sixth would have to be put together in a hurry, and we were both tired from two months travel. My faith in God did not waver, but I had much less faith in my own ability to continue. So we brought to a close our first memorable crusade.

The next year, 1962, the Committee on Evangelism assigned us to a second crusade over the same route. And the memory of the crowds that came in 1961 led to a lot of exaggerated advertising by the local people – just as people like to do with successful evangelists in other countries.

It really concerned me, because I considered such publicity tantamount to taking credit for a great work that the Spirit of God had done. Moreover, I didn't want to agitate the 95% Muslim community in Indonesia. Therefore, I appealed to them not to do it!

While I was in Surabaya on the first crusade, I met some of my old high school buddies who had known me in school, when I was a devout Buddhist.

"When in the world did you switch religion?" they asked, slapping me on the back. Some of them even came to the meetings. Out of curiosity, I suppose.

"How did a rascal like you ever turn into a saint and a prophet in such a short time?" I was asked. I was not sure that I liked that comment, and stiffly reminded them that it was 12 years ago that we were in high school. Besides that, I did not claim to be either saint or prophet.

I was sorry later to have replied that way, because it dawned on me that my sudden appearance as a Christian evangelist might help bring about the conversion of some of my old friends. One of them, I know, did accept Christ. He told me, "People come to me now to ask about you, because they have heard I knew you in school. How can I convince them what a mischief-maker you were? They'll just think I was bragging when I said I knew you, and was lying all the time."

He laughed as he walked away. And then he added, "Look for me at your meetings next year. I'll be there." He was. By then he was already a Christian. ✟

Chapter 8

New Horizons

While in Australia, I joined the Overseas Christian Fellowship, in order to continue our Christian contacts with the young men and women studying among us there. What I could not have known, at the time, was that this simple decision would lead to a major change in the course of our whole life, and in the direction of our ministry.

In October 1962, almost three years after we graduated from the Bible College in Adelaide, I began to receive letters from other Asian Christians in various countries – ministers whom I had known as graduate students in Australia – inviting me to speak at Christian conferences in Southeast Asia and other parts of the Far East. It was impossible for us to travel abroad from Indonesia freely, because of the strict control of foreign exchange. Fortunately, our friends abroad were aware of these financial barriers, so each invitation was accompanied by an offer to pay travel costs.

Debbie and I became more and more excited over the prospect of "escaping" for a time the severe restrictions on travel by Chinese-Indonesians. We were also elated over the chance to meet our friends again, and to see what Asian Christians were doing in other countries. So we looked over our invitations and found it was possible to schedule them, one after another, over a period of six months. Thus we started, in October 1962, a trip that was to change our lives.

In preparation for the trip, I polished my English by listening to the Voice of America (VOA) program in "special (simple) English," broadcast daily from Washington, D.C. I listened to it intensely, fearing that my English was evaporating from lack of use. If I had known that within one year I would be broadcasting from Washington, D.C., I might have died from eager anticipation. It was during those hours of listening to VOA that I began to dream of the vast harvest of souls that could be brought into Christ's kingdom if a Christian message could be broadcast to Indonesia.

But I brushed aside the dream. It was impossible. Yet, in the back of my mind I was convinced that radio would be the perfect solution to the difficulties facing Christian missionaries and Christian ministers in Indonesia.

Under the communist-dominated Sukarno regime travel, even between the islands, was nearly impossible. Many were in rebellion against Sukarno. Mail was censored. All tapes found in the mail were confiscated. Travel permits were hard to get, even harder if you happened to be of Chinese extraction.

The first stop on our Asian odyssey was the Federation of Malaysia and Singapore, where English was spoken. There I could speak and preach without interpretation, thanks to the VOA (By coincidence, the VOA broadcaster at that time was Forrest Boyd, who later became a close friend as a member of Fourth Presbyterian Church in Washington, D.C.).

We moved ahead on schedule, keeping all our engagements to lecture at theological schools and colleges, to preach at Christian crusades, and to attend church conferences. Our schedule took us through Thailand, then to Hong Kong. It was in Hong Kong where the shape of things to come was first revealed to us. But we did not think of it then as a prophetic occurrence. What happened was this: we met the Hong Kong manager of the Far East Broadcasting Company (FEBC), a missionary whose job it was to get the Christian message into communist China. He seized the opportunity of our visit – noting that we were Chinese – to ask us to make some tapes of sermons and songs for his radio station.

I had to explain to him that it was Debbie who was fluent in Chinese, and that I had learned what I knew of it from her. So it came about that Debbie was the star of these early efforts of the Swieson family as Christian broadcasters. She taped several talks in Chinese, and sang religious songs. They were broadcast after we left, but the experience was exciting. It couldn't have come at a better time. For at our next stop, in Manila, we were invited to have a look at the FEBC studios, a missionary institution. By fortunate "coincidence" Robert Bowman, president of the company, was there on a visit. He began urging us to switch to a radio ministry. Before we knew what was happening, he had talked us into thinking seriously about making some experimental Christian broadcasts for his station. He was a high-pressure salesman.

He explained it was impossible to get tapes to or from Indonesia. They were being "lost" in the mails, on orders of the censors.

"The only way to get the Gospel to your country," he said, "is by radio. When we go in on the airwaves, we can reach every one of your 3000 islands. There is no way to put a wall to keep us out."

He exhorted us to be brave, and step into a new broadcasting career without fear. He guaranteed that if we would agree to supply his station with tapes in the native Indonesian Malay language, he would see they were broadcast to the people who need the message of Christ.

It was tempting! So tempting! We even talked of abandoning the rest of our trip, and switching to a broadcast ministry, right then and there. In my dreams about broadcasting, I had always counted on a long, hard struggle to get a start. And there I was having such an offer laid in my lap. Why hesitate now? But every time we leaned toward accepting his offer at once, the voices of our conscience reminded us that we had made promises to the friends who were paying for our trip. Should we break our promises? No!

So, in the end, we agreed to make a dozen experimental tapes while we were there, to see if we could do it, if the station liked what we did, and how the listeners would respond.

Debbie sang at the opening of each program. I spoke briefly, usually about 10 minutes. Then the program closed with more singing by Debbie. For me, the toughest part was to keep from talking too long. I ran overtime on several tapes, and we had to do them over again. They had to fit exactly into the number of allotted minutes, not a second longer. It was great discipline for me. It forced me to organize my thoughts better than I had ever done before, and to be more precise in expressing them.

Finally we completed a dozen tapes, each about 15 minutes long. We gave them to the station staff the day we left, and they told us they would start broadcasting them at once. So we left for a rather lengthy visit to Japan to carry out our promises, and within a few days we had all but forgotten the 12 taped Christian broadcasts we had left in Manila.

We were genuinely surprised, a few weeks later, to get a phone call from Bob Bowman at our hotel in Tokyo. He had just arrived from Manila, and told us he had terrific news! "How soon can I talk to you?" he said. "How about right now? If you can't come to my hotel, I'll get to yours."

The urgency in his voice was exciting! We told him we would come to his hotel, as soon as we changed our clothes.

In the lobby of his hotel, the Marunouchi, Bob gave us his exciting report. Our tapes were a smashing success, he said. They were so successful, he went on, that the station was being swamped with mail, praising the programs and demanding to know the identity of this new speaker and his wife. "You've just got to join us now," he urged. "It's not just Bob Bowman speaking now, it's the radio audience of all of southeastern Asia! They want to hear you both. Debbie's singing was a hit. She drew many listeners who would not have tuned in to an all-talk show."

Still we wavered. We explored the possibilities in depth. Bob took the historical view. Because of the unfortunate restriction of liberties by Sukarno, he argued, we have a wonderful opportunity for a massive ministry by radio, at this particular time.

"Don't let this chance slip by," he pleaded. "There is no other way to bring Indonesia to Christ, under the rule of a dictator." He was expressing the very arguments that I had been making to myself.

If I returned to Indonesia, my ministry would be confined to the island of Java. I knew that there was a vast audience of shortwave owners in the islands. Bob reminded us that there were millions in Singapore and Malay states and Brunei, and in other islands near Indonesia who speak the Indonesian Malay language.

He explained that the way they judged the total number of listeners was by the number of letters received. Because of the widespread poverty in the area, they figured that one letter received represented 1000 listeners. The other 999 were either too poor to pay the postage – which cost as much as a plate of rice – or too uneducated to write.

Still I hesitated. I remembered the thrill of preaching to the vast, overflowing audiences on the Java crusades, and seeing and hearing them as they gave their lives to Christ. As a radio preacher I would disappear from public view, and even my name would cease to be known. On the air I would be only "a voice without a name". Even without Bob's assurance that God would know me, even if the world didn't, it was a difficult decision to make.

It was, in effect, obeying a call to anonymity. I desired to be known, as would any other human being. But I knew, too, that it would cripple my radio ministry if I gave my name, for if the millions in Asia who despise the Chinese for their business talents and prosperity, heard that I was one of "those Chinese," they would turn me off, and probably turn Christ off, too.

There was no chance of getting permission to make Christian broadcasts from stations inside Indonesia. They were all government-owned, dominated by the ruling pro-communist faction.

The thought that I would leave Indonesia, and possibly never go back again, brought a wave of sadness

in the midst of the exciting thoughts about this new
career. There was a special sadness for me, in the
thought that I might never see my beloved mother again
– the mother to whom I owed my life and health.

As I wavered, the Lord led me to meet with Dr.
Gordon Chapman, a Presbyterian missionary and a
great man of God. He promptly joined the others in
urging me to make the change, to forget the anonymity
of the job and the obscurity that was necessary.
"Remember," he said, "God will know what you are
doing."

So after fervent prayer, Debbie and I finally said
"yes."

As we pondered where to have our base of
operations, Dr. Chapman suggested the Fourth
Presbyterian Church, in Washington, D.C. He gave two
reasons. First, because the pastor was the Rev. Richard
C. Halverson, a man with a worldwide vision of the
ministry of the Gospel, and a special stake in that
ministry through his leadership of the World Vision
movement. Second, because Fourth Church already had
a radio ministry. It was broadcasting its Sunday
morning services, through a fully equipped studio in the
church. And the studio was not used during the week,
so should be available to me.

We checked this with our missionary friends,
receiving unanimous approval. Our minds were made
up. The United States was the place to go.

But how to get there? It was 7000 miles to the
Pacific coast, and 3000 miles further to Washington. So
we had a financial problem now. But we went ahead,
gathering letters of introduction to Dr. Halverson and
others. Then, as we thought we'd better start consulting
the Lord about money problems, Debbie came through
with the solution! "I will ask my brother, Ban," she said.

Why The Angels Laughed

Now Ban, of all the 11 brothers and sisters in Debbie's big family, was my favorite. When there was no father to give Debbie away at our wedding, brother Ban stood in.

He was not a Christian at that time, but was the only one of Debbie's non-Christian family members who always asked me to pray at mealtime. He said he admired my choice of a life work. At this important juncture, he was operating an import-export business overseas, well beyond Sukarno's exchange controls.

Brother Ban, who lived in Hong Kong at that time, came through in our money crisis, as he had helped in other troubles. He provided all the financial help we needed. We hadn't even had time to think of a possible alternative source, when his money order came. And with it he sent his wishes for success in our new ministry and our new country. He said his prayers would go with us. Ban's telegram removed the last doubt and the final barrier. We took off for the United States, firm in our faith we were doing what God wanted us to do.

Ban died of a heart attack behind the wheel of a car in Australia in 1975. I believe he was a Christian at the end. While he was still a sort of Buddhist, so far as the public was concerned, he was following the teachings of Christ. When his wife, Kym, phoned us of his death from Australia, I expressed confidence that we would meet him again, in heaven. He was truly a good, kind, compassionate and charitable man. I'm sure that Jesus loved him. ✝

Chapter 9

The Voice Without a Name

Our soaring hopes and expanding motivation, to launch a radio ministry that would shake the Asian world, were suddenly deflated when we landed in California. What a country! The confusion of roaring expressways, flashing red and green lights, signs that said "walk" when we wanted to stop for a moment and look, then flashed to "don't walk" just as we got ready to move on. People rushing past in both directions, obviously in such a hurry we didn't dare stop them to ask directions. Buildings that poked through the clouds, and taxi fares even higher. It was all frightening, and made us feel very small and a little lonely. We wondered, that first day in America, if we would ever feel at home in this land of, what seemed to us, deliberately organized disorder, or carefully created chaos. How to do God's work in such confusion?

But, as we flew east, America came into focus. There was a sweep and grandeur in the mountains, the deep gorges, the deserts and plains, and the glistening little cities that seemed to be in parade as we passed over. The beautiful young hostesses were extra kind to us. We had expected to be shunned, having heard of the prejudice against Asians. So it was a happy surprise when an executive-looking Caucasian leaned across the aisle to offer a good view of the Grand Canyon from his side of the airplane. Though we never spoke without first being spoken to, we found ourselves telling about our prospective new work to several on the cross-country flight. One of them confided that he, too, was active in church work, and we talked about the difficulties of the churches in revolutionary Indonesia. Our hearts quickly warmed to these friendly people. But still we wondered. Have we made a mistake in choosing to work in America? It is so big. And we are so small.

All doubts vanished when we landed in Washington. Dr. Halverson greeted us with a friendly handshake and a brotherly hug. He had been briefed in detail about our plans, and assured us that the radio room at the church was ours to use. He wiped out the last vestiges of our worry when he told us the church wanted to support us as its own missionaries! And he took us to temporary quarters prepared for us. Suddenly we knew that we were at home! We were swimming in an ocean of Christian love! We wept a little, out of pure happiness, then knelt and asked the Lord to forgive our doubts and fears, and to strengthen our faith.

After that happy start, things got better and better. At the studio on our first day we found an expert producer – a real perfectionist – Edward Walker, of a local radio station, waiting to work with us. He had music ready for the early tapes. One of his favorites was Ted Smith, a member of Fourth Church and Billy Graham's pianist, whose recordings soon became popular in Asia through our programs. Glenn Kirkland, a scientist at Johns Hopkins University, lent us his expertise in radio engineering. Finally, by September 1963, we were ready to start.

At first, we put together two taped programs a week, and sent them by air mail to FEBC radio station in Manila. They were beamed to areas where Indonesian and Chinese were understood.

The staff in Manila was swamped with mail from listeners. So at the end of the first six months we added a third program weekly. And we started a question-and-answer program, concentrating on the questions most often asked about this strange new religion called Christianity.

We never gave our Washington address on the air, nor told our listeners that it was Eddy Swieson talking. But we were tempted. I am as fond of praise and fame as anyone, and it was tough to remain anonymous with so many listeners asking for autographed photos, or at least the identity of "the voice without a name."

Officials of Asiatic governments wrote on fine stationery, asking who was doing the preaching. University students sent fan letters to the unknown voice written on lined notebook paper. Others, too poor to buy writing pads, sent letters written on pieces of brown paper bags. The pressure grew. I was tempted again and again to give my name – maybe just once – and to tell them how the programs reached them from Washington.

But I prayed about it, and the Lord laid a steadying hand on my shoulder. I was reminded, again, of the prejudice that millions in Asia hold against my race, and also against the Dutch Reformed Church that was my affiliation in the body of Christ.

The Lord seemed to be saying, "Steady, Eddy. You're doing just fine. Keep on as you are. Maybe the world doesn't know you, but I do."

To attract the more sophisticated listeners, we "baited" our programs with interludes of classical music, and religious and popular songs, both before and after the sermon. We also deliberately complimented our listeners' intelligence by using English words now and then, somewhat Indonesianized, as if to say that we were sure they were smart enough to know what the words meant. Sukarno used the same tactic in his rise to power.

By trial and error, and by reading the mail, we found what the listeners like in music, and what interested, or puzzled them most about the Gospel. And we emphasized these things.

After three years, we made a listener survey. It was clear that the "Indonesian News of Hope" programs had "arrived." Our audience was estimated at no less than three million. Between September 1963 and early 1970 when the final program was taped, we had preached and sung and played music for our vast congregation more than 400 times – as recorded on 400 separate tapes.

Now and then – probably 20 or 30 times – Debbie had starred in her own taped programs in Mandarin Chinese, both preaching and singing for listeners in mainland China.

But the end of the taping did not end the broadcasts. With letters of enthusiasm still pouring in, the Manila station started re-running the tapes. For six years after the last tape was produced in 1970, the "voice without a name" spoke out on its regular weekly schedule from Manila. No one seemed to notice, at least they didn't complain, that they had heard the same words some years before. There were enough tapes so that it was unnecessary to repeat any program oftener than every 2 or 3 years.

Finally, the Manila broadcasters called for help.

"We still have your program on our schedule," they wrote. "It is being beamed to Indonesia and Malaysia. The musical and question-and-answer tapes have been taken off because we are not getting any new tapes from you. But we are planning to continue the sermon and musical programs on our Indonesian schedule for the 1976 season. You will note that all are on three prime times, with the family as the intended audience. All have been aired several times now, and we certainly need some fresh programs to keep us going."

To add a little pressure to their argument, the broadcasters sent me a few sample letters. A youth from Malaysia wrote, "At last I have found salvation! Jesus Christ came to save me and died for my sins. What a wonderful Savior! FEBC has saved countless souls, and I am one of them. I thank you very much."

A listener from Pakistan said, "Being a Muslim I should not care to listen to your programs, but this is not the case with me. In my own views I have the same respect for Christianity, so I am listening regularly to the sweet voice of Jesus. I have gained a lot of knowledge through your different programs. I like the programs about the Lord most. I am very eager to know more, and in detail, about Jesus."

I read these letters with mixed feelings of joy and sadness. Joy because my broadcasts were still bearing fruit. Sadness because in my heart I knew it was impossible, and maybe even unnecessary, to produce a new series of tapes of the voice without a name. Even while still broadcasting, I had gratefully accepted the offer to become assistant pastor of the Fourth Presbyterian Church. When the period of broadcasting came to an end, Dr. Halverson had asked me to take on additional ministry to reach people for Christ here in America. One of them was to help Lee Campbell, a member of Fourth Church, who had launched a teaching and discipleship work known as Community Bible Study. I was asked to take the role of curricula/ commentary writer for the first five years of this new mission. How could I add a schedule of broadcasting to this?

But there is still another reason for the voice without a name to be allowed to fall silent. There was now a fast-growing crop of active, eager young Christian ministers in Indonesia. Under the new Suharto government there were few restrictions on travel, freedom of speech, and freedom of worship. The time of oppression was past. The Word of God now could be preached face to face to people who needed to hear it.

So the voice without a name will not return. And to preserve whatever good the programs did, in their day, the voice will never be identified.

In a Christmas party held at the Indonesian Embassy in Washington, D.C., the Indonesian Ambassador who knew me invited me to give a short message on the significance of Christmas!

I recall, during the reception that followed, a member of the ambassador's diplomatic staff looked me over curiously. "Isn't it rather remarkable that you, an Asian, are preaching at this big American church?" he asked.

I thanked him for what I knew he intended as a compliment, though there seemed to be undertones of doubt about the fitness of an Asian to handle such a job. "The Lord has been very good to me," I said. "He has given me opportunities for service to Him far above and beyond what I ever dreamed would be possible."

The man looked at me in a strange way again and said, with a question in his voice: "We must have met before, I don't recall your face, but your voice is very familiar to me. I'm sure we must have talked together.

Possibly by phone, and not too long ago. I'm pretty good at remembering voices, although I don't always attach names to them."

"No," I replied. "I don't think we have ever met. We have been living in America now for more than a decade, and have become American citizens. So, if this is your first visit to the United States, as you say, then it surely is not possible that we have met. There must be another voice somewhere in Indonesia that sounds like mine." I shook his hand, wished him well, and moved on to another group of guests.

When I turned and looked back, the diplomat was still looking after me with a puzzled expression. A few moments later, while I was talking with an American friend, there was a gentle tap on my shoulder, and there, standing behind me with a triumphant smile on his face, was the same gentleman.

"I've got it!" he burst out. "I know who you are! You are the 'voice without a name.' You are the Indonesian News of Hope broadcaster! That must be it. You are a minister, and the News of Hope broadcaster was a preacher of sermons. Your voice and his voice sound exactly the same. I have listened often. I like your music. That girl who sings. Who is she? Is she your wife, or maybe your daughter? Now, am I right? I know it has been a secret, but I think I have solved it. Tell me, are you the voice without a name?"

I smiled and tried to put a surprised and doubtful look on my face, but couldn't hold it. I finally broke into laughter. "You would make a great detective," I said. "Yes, I will confess, now that you have cornered me. After all, as a Christian minister I cannot tell outright lies, and should not even give false impressions. I was the voice, several years ago."

"Was?" he questioned. "But I heard you only last month, before I left Indonesia on this tour. Is there now an imposter taking your place?" Then, after a moment pondering, he asked, "If you have been living in America so long, when did you do your broadcasting? I suppose we are listening to some of your old records now?"

So I told him the whole story, of how we had moved to America because of oppression that blocked the sending of tapes out of Indonesia for broadcasting back to our country. I explained that "the voice" had always come from Washington, D.C., never live from Manila. And I assured him that the lovely lady, whose singing he admired, was my wife, not my daughter.

"But why all the hush-hush secrecy about it?", he asked. "Why didn't you announce your name? By now you would be famous all over Asia. You are a pretty good preacher. Were you ashamed of your job? Or didn't your boss allow you to give your name?"

I chuckled a bit and then nodded: "You have guessed it again," I said. "My boss thought it best for me to remain anonymous." In my thoughts I silently asked the Lord to forgive me for skirting the truth and calling Him "boss."

And then I added, "I was born in Indonesia, but I am Chinese. And you know how many of our people have unkind opinions of us. If I had given you my Chinese name, instead of only the sound of my voice, would you have listened to me? Would all the mixed nationalities and religions of our homeland have listened? To a native Indonesian, probably. To an Indonesian with a Chinese name, no! The 'boss' was obviously right in keeping my name out of the picture."

"Humpf," my friend commented. "I'd never work for a boss like that!"

I shook his hand, as I started to move off, and replied, "I think you would."✟

Chapter 10

The Challenge

After working two years in Washington at my broadcasting job, I received a telephone call that left me stunned. It came from Dr. Halverson, and was to the point. "Eddy," he said, "I want you to become assistant pastor of Fourth Church."

Earlier that day the dentist extracted my impacted wisdom teeth. My guess is, the trauma I suffered in the dentist office and the surprising call from Dr. Halverson caused me to stammer and stutter, and the words wouldn't come. Before I could pull myself together sufficiently to make an intelligent reply, Dr. Halverson interrupted with another generous offer. "It's fine with us if you want to continue with your broadcasting," he said.

When I recovered sufficiently to put together a sensible sentence of thanks, and an expression of my deep appreciation for his amazing faith in a young Asian who had not yet done enough preaching in English to be confident of doing it on a regular basis, the pastor cut me off with an expression of thanks for my willingness to assume this extra burden of work.

"Burden!" I thought. "How many thousands of young preachers pray every night to be offered such a burden!"

My head was in a whirl, but I had the presence of mind to tell Debbie, so she wouldn't think I was having some kind of a seizure. Then I sought out a chair, out of breath and limp with suppressed excitement.

This was unheard of! An Asian, not anywhere near the point of becoming an American citizen, ministering to a 98% white Caucasian church. Will this sophisticated congregation accept me as their minister? Although I had, frankly, not seen much of the alleged prejudice against Asians since my arrival in America, I knew it was there. And I wondered.

One of my earliest friends in the church, the late Samuel B. Coleman, was frank in his assessment of my situation and in his advice to me. "Eddy," he said, "you're in a tough spot. This is a very affluent community. There are a lot of government officials, Congressmen, Senators and a number of the President's cabinet members. And yes, there are also highly educated professionals among us. You will have to study and study and study. You must increase your knowledge, as fast as you can. You must sharpen your sensitivity, and always present yourself neat and clean."

I was scared. But it didn't take long for the love of this great congregation to surround and comfort me.

When the word got out that I was to be the new assistant pastor, a prominent member of the church came to my home and knocked on the door. When I opened it, he took me by the arm, led me to the curb, and presented me with the keys to the car that was parked there.

"You're going to need it," was his only comment. I did.

For the first months as assistant pastor I hardly dared open my mouth. I made a practice of never saying anything that anybody was likely to disagree with.

Our American friends continued to shower us with shining examples of Christian love and concern. One couple, learning that we were moving into an apartment and had little furniture, told us they wanted to take us for a drive one afternoon. They drove directly to a lovely furniture store, and told us to pick the furniture we needed for kitchen, living room, and study room. And they paid for it. Later, the wives went shopping. Debbie came home with the most useful domestic tool of all, a sewing machine. It was paid for by our friends.

I was still a member of the Indonesian Reformed Church when I arrived in Washington. After experiencing the love and concern of the people of the Fourth Presbyterian Church, I had an overwhelming urge to join the church and thus come into closer fellowship with them. I was told the procedure was simple. All I had to do was ask the Reformed Synod in Indonesia to transfer my membership to the Washington City Presbytery of the United Presbyterian Church (U.S.A.). Both churches are members of the World Presbyterian Alliance so, I was told, there would be no problem.

But nobody in Washington had ever tackled such a transfer. It was of course, my first try at it, too.

It was months before the messages back and forth over the 10,000 miles to Indonesia verified who I was, and that the Washington Presbytery could rest assured that as an ordained minister of the Reformed Synod of Java, I would preach only Jesus Christ, and Him crucified.

Americans are very self-assertive. In fact, from the viewpoint of an Asian just in from Asia, they seemed downright aggressive. But my fears took a positive turn. They convinced me that Mr. Coleman was right. I needed more education.

I was determined to learn everything I could cram into my head about Western thought and Western civilization. But while learning, I remained cautious, working all sorts of strategies to avoid embarrassment.

For example, when asked by someone to make a visit to a hospitalized member of the congregation, I would first call by telephone, explain who I was, and ask them if they would like me to talk with them, pray with them, and share the Scriptures. Wonder of all wonders to me, in all the years that I ministered to this congregation, not a single door was slammed in the face of this Asian.

My only frustrations were due to my personal habits and disposition, my fear of being candid, my Asian shyness and politeness. I still remember the day I first determined that it was foolish to continue this shyness and reserve.

Shortly thereafter, I was standing outside the church after a service, thinking of some problem, and must have been wearing an expression of concern on my face. A nice looking gentleman was walking by, and took a piercing look at me. He turned around and slapped me on the back, jolting me out of my worried trance. He said, "Eddy, relax. We all love you." The gentleman turned out to be U.S. Senator Mark O. Hatfield. He shared with me how he was often inspired by my opening invocations. His comment was so efficacious, helping to reduce my fear of being ineffective in this unique congregation. In fact, on several occasions the Senator invited me to the Capitol to pray with him. But my greatest surprise came later, when Senator Hatfield was the main speaker at my graduation!

One of the most thrilling and deeply emotional events for us was when Debbie and I became United States citizens on October 16, 1970 in the Sixth Judicial Circuit Court in Montgomery County, Maryland. Many of our friends from Fourth Presbyterian Church, including the late Mr. Frank Sanders, the Assistant Secretary of the Navy, were present for this momentous occasion.

After we solemnly pledged before Judge Kathryn J. Shook, that we were ready to relinquish all allegiance to our former motherland, and were willing to pledge allegiance to the United States of America, and to serve whenever and wherever we were called to do so, we were officially pronounced citizens of this country.

Before we were dismissed, Judge Shook gave some closing remarks. She admitted that when she heard us saying the Pledge of Allegiance and saw our faces in that courtroom, she simply couldn't hold back her tears of emotion. Neither could I, nor presumably a few others who went through that solemn ceremony. The special moment was when the judge read both my original Chinese name, Eddy Swiesing Ie, and my new name, Eddy I. Swieson. I remember hearing applause among the audience, and knew it came from my Fourth Church friends.

The next day, to my surprise, a "special delivery" package came from the U.S. Capitol, addressed to Eddy Swieson. It was the very American flag that was flown on the Capitol building the day we were naturalized! A note was included to congratulate and welcome us to a new family. That flag has become one of the most cherished decorations in my office.

I would be remiss not to share my deep emotional moments during the citizenship orientation, when we were exposed to both American history and the Constitution created by our founding fathers. Having come from an oppressive political background, and now being introduced to such remarkable freedom and individual responsibility in America, I was ready and enthusiastic to offer myself for any service needed here or abroad. In fact, I went immediately to sign up at the Selective Service office, and told the officer that I was willing to serve as a military chaplain whenever they needed me.

Having great respect for Mr. Coleman, I was determined to follow his advice and increase my knowledge. So I enrolled at George Washington University to study in my off hours. Later, I took courses for two years at the American University School of International Service. Then, from 1971 to 1974 I studied for a doctorate at the Wesley Theological Seminary in Washington. My long search for knowledge reached a high point when I was awarded my Doctorate of Ministry from the Wesley Seminary, with a specialization in World Missions.

One of the most heartwarming moments of my life in America was the first time that, as Dr. Eddy Swieson, I wore in the pulpit the robe and insignia that signified the new ecclesiastical rank. Everyone in the congregation knew how long and hard I had studied to earn it. So there was a spontaneous burst of applause in the packed sanctuary of that "sophisticated" 150-year-old church.

Study has been my source of "fun" throughout my life. The doctorate was not my goal, only a marker on the way to the goal. My path to that goal takes a lifetime of study to completely achieve.

Languages are my favorite study. To qualify as a Bible scholar of sufficient insight to prepare commentaries for the rapid growing Community Bible Study which Lee Campbell spearheaded, I sought to acquire a working knowledge of Greek and Hebrew, spending as many Monday nights as possible at the Jewish Community Center to improve my conversational Hebrew.

In the course of my career as a student in Indonesia and Australia, I have been obliged to learn Indonesian, Mandarin Chinese, Dutch, and English, and also to keep brushed up on my reading knowledge of German. Now my latest project was to master the "American" language, to help me communicate with the "career singles" of our church. Dr. Halverson assigned me to provide good Bible teaching to them. Within less than one year, the group had grown to nearly 600 people, meeting every Sunday morning from 8:30 to 10:00. Since there was no room for such a large class on Fourth Church campus, we met in the ballroom of a nearby Holiday Inn.

Fourth Church, despite its large and growing congregation, was a happy church that liked to laugh. Even in the midst of the deadly serious work for the Lord, we seemed to find a lot to laugh about.

A telephone call that came to my office will illustrate. The voice on the telephone said, "Hooray for Fourth Church! You finally got yourselves a real Scottish Presbyterian preacher! I just heard him on the radio, and he's great! Nothing like a good, solid Presbyterian Scot to put the Gospel in words you can understand...."

The secretary interrupted politely, "Sir?" As my caller ignored the interruption and talked on, she said again, "Sir? I think the man you are referring to is Dr. Eddy Swieson, and he...."

"Yeah, that's the name. I couldn't mistake that good Scottish accent, even before I heard the name...."

I had already pressed the button and was listening as this exchange continued.

"Well, sir," the secretary interrupted again, "Dr. Swieson is not Scottish, you see. We do think he is a fine preacher, but he is, in fact, Chinese. He was born in Java, and brought up as a Buddhist...."

There was silence on the other end of the line, so the secretary checked to see if the caller was still there." "Sir?" "Sir, are you there?"

This time it was the caller who interrupted. "I don't believe it," he said. The phone clicked dead. The secretary sighed and then, noting that I was on the line, she chuckled and said, "Eddy, that was another one." For this was not the first caller to be misled by my name and accent.

Shortly after coming to Fourth Church, I had a similar case of wrong identification. A call came one morning from a man who said he was an Episcopalian, and wanted me to officiate at his wedding. I readily agreed to do it, but was curious as to why an Episcopalian wanted a Presbyterian minister.

The reason he wanted me, he said, was that he and his future bride had heard me preach on the radio and were impressed by my sermon. And besides, he added, " I am marrying a Presbyterian."

I gave him the usual explanation of my requirement of a face-to-face meeting with each couple before the ceremony, to get acquainted and give me an opportunity to ask questions. He readily agreed that this was a reasonable request.

We talked by phone several more times, making the arrangements for the wedding, and finally set a date for the interview.

At the appointed time there was a knock on my door. Fortunately, I was wearing my clerical collar that day, and opened the door myself. The man shook hands with me and said that he had an appointment with Dr. Swieson.

"Well, I'm glad to see you." "I'm Dr. Swieson."

Well, that man stood as if paralyzed, and his face turned pale. He looked like he had seen a ghost. His jaw dropped and his eyes popped wide open. For a moment I thought he might be having a seizure. But he recovered quickly, and we sat down and the three of us had a good conversation. But I was curious, so just as he was leaving I asked him whether he had been sick, or what was the matter when he first arrived. "You looked very pale and shaken," I said.

He blushed and looked at his lady, and then it came out. "I almost dropped dead," he said. "You can see that I'm Scandinavian, and you have a Scandinavian name, or one that sounds Scandinavian. Since you have a definite Swedish accent on the radio, I thought you were one of my countrymen, and that it would be nice to be married by someone from the home country. So I guess you can understand my reaction when Dr. Swieson turned out to be a Chinese in clerical collar!"

By this time, my fear of not being accepted by members and friends of Fourth Church was pretty well eradicated. Another strong confirmation came from Mr. J. William Middendorf II, the Secretary of the Navy. He and his wife frequently attended my biblical linguistic class. One day he wrote me a letter, inviting me to participate in christening the newly built USS Saipan

LHA-2 in Pascagoula, Mississippi. Like the stunning telephone call from Dr. Halverson in June 1965, asking me to be his assistant, I was once more overwhelmed. God used this invitation to give me greater confidence in His sovereign grace for the greater challenge ahead.

One of the unforgettable embarrassments of my married life was when our son, Dana, was born after eight years of marriage. It was such a happy event, especially since it was so long delayed. But the events surrounding the birth were nearly too embarrassing to tell about them.

When I first arrived in America, and was shown through an American hospital and saw the miraculous work done by the American doctors, I acquired a great faith in their skill. I had spent a good part of my life being doctored by my mother, with substitute remedies she concocted herself, when medicines were not available. So it gave me a secure feeling to be in a country where there was no limit to what the doctors could do, and no scarcity of medicines or equipment.

So, when Debbie became pregnant, and the doctors solemnly informed us that the baby would arrive toward the end of May or in June, I felt that my wife had no right to start complaining of birth pangs on April 12. I told her it was probably just stomach cramps, that it couldn't be anything else. Then I gave her a glass of water and an aspirin and advised her to go back to sleep.

An hour later she shook me awake again. "Eddy," she said, "I'm sure these are birth pains, and they are coming more often."

"Honey," I explained, "the doctor said 'end of May or early June' and this is only April 12. You can't be seven weeks early. It's bound to go away. Where is your faith in our well-trained doctors? So take another aspirin, or maybe a glass of milk. We've got to get some sleep."

When she got up the next morning, very early, she was still having pains, but I was still confident that these American doctors knew what they were talking about. So I prepared to go to the church office.

Debbie wasn't convinced. While I was dressing, she called the doctor, and he told her to come to the hospital right away. So, still laughing in a superior way and certain it was all a false alarm, I drove her to the hospital, dropped her off in front of the elevator, and left for my office, instructing her to call me when she was ready to return home.

About 2:00 p.m. my office phone rang. It was the voice of a nurse in the baby ward.

"You have a fine baby son, and your wife is just fine, too." she said. Finally, I gathered my senses together and answered, "Oh!" That was all.

All the way to the hospital, at speeds much beyond the limit, I was still suspicious that Debbie had put the nurse up to this, that it was all a practical joke. I refused to believe it until I got to the hospital and felt that tiny hand grasp my finger. It was then that I wept. Tears of happiness.

Returning to my office from the hospital and sharing the good news, I was severely chastised by our senior church secretary, Ms. Evelyn Webb, for being so skeptical and insensitive to Debbie.

And in all that excitement, sad to say, it was not until late that night that I remembered I had not knelt and thanked the Lord Jesus for giving us this precious gift.

In 1980 Dr. Halverson was leaving his position as senior pastor at Fourth to become Chaplain of the United States Senate.

Two years later, I received a call to serve as the founding pastor of a non-denominational congregation, Christian Covenant Church in Rockville, Maryland.

During my 15 years of ministry as the senior pastor, I often recalled my early motto, "I do not consider the doctorate a goal. To reach that goal will take a lifetime of learning."

The Lord's goodness was shown to me through the growth and maturing of this young congregation until the day I retired from the pastorate in the Fall of 1997. An able young evangelist, Greg Zetts, was called by the board to succeed me. ✝

Chapter 11

My Dream to be Adopted

An aged man, his body painfully twisted by crippling rheumatism, was wheeled into a tiny room in the courthouse in the town of Mojokerto, on the island of Java. It was September 18, 1974.

The court clerk cleared his throat, shuffled through a handful of legal papers, then looked over his glasses at the small group of men and women surrounding the wheelchair.

"Is this man Mr. Indro Imanjaja, formerly known as Mr. Ie IkDjoen, a citizen of Indonesia?" he inquired in his customary impersonal monotone. The old man stared a moment, with uncomprehending eyes, then nodded as he recognized his name.

"You are the father of one Eddy Ie Swieson, formerly known as Ie Swie Sing, now serving as associate pastor of the Fourth Presbyterian Church in Washington, D.C.", the clerk droned on.

105

The old man's eyes brightened for an instant, almost imperceptibly, at the sound of his son's name. He nodded again, affirmatively.

"Does this man understand the significance of these proceedings?" the clerk inquired, turning to the group standing beside the wheelchair. "Is he able to talk? Can he understand the oath and sign his name?"

"He can understand, sir," one of the group replied. "But he is very weak and in much pain, so he cannot move his hands sufficiently to sign his name. But we have been told his fingerprint will do just well."

"Very well," the clerk said, looking at the papers in his hands. "Then, let's proceed. Am I to understand that this son was born on November 28, 1932 at Mojotrisno, East Java, Indonesia? We are speaking now of Mr. Eddy Ie Swieson."

The stooped, gray head peered up from the wheelchair and nodded.

"Now, according to these documents, your wife, the real mother of Mr. Eddy Ie Swieson died some years ago. Let's see, the date, I believe, is October 5, 1953. Is that correct?" Once again, the old man nodded.

"This means, then, that you are the only surviving parent of said Eddy Ie Swieson?"

"That's right, sir," one of the group spoke up. "But may I say, again, that Mr. Imanjaja is in great pain, and it would be a kindness if we could move ahead as rapidly as possible."

"I understand," the clerk said, without altering his official frown. "But there are certain things that must be made clear. Judging by the age of the persons involved, this case must have been pending for quite a long time, and I think we can all afford a few extra moments to make sure everything is in order."

Then, looking back at his papers, he went on, "These documents state that Mr. Imanjaja surrendered the above-mentioned son, Mr. Eddy Ie Swieson, to the care of Mrs. Rini Tan, a housewife residing at Mojokerto, East Java, Indonesia, and that she is the wife of the deceased Jusuf Pilemon Imanjaja. Is this, too, correct?"

The man in the wheelchair nodded again. His eyes were closed. The clerk glanced at the crippled figure, and his words began to come faster.

"We must also confirm that Mrs. Rini Tan and Mr. Jusuh Pilemon Imanjaja both obtained these new names based on the decision of the presidential cabinet of the Republic of Indonesia, Number 127/U/Kep/12/ 1966, accepted and approved by the mayor of the city of Surabaya on August 5, 1967. The Registered Number is 3911/Gt/Nm/Komad/1967L, which has been shown to me." Looking over his glasses toward the wheelchair, he turned quickly to his reading, even before the old man could nod his approval.

"The death certificate of Mr. Jusuf Pilemon has been shown to me, so we can skip the certification there. But now, this is an important point: In addition to expressing his consent, the one who appears before me here today," he nodded in the direction of the wheelchair, "also indicates his desire to convey to Mrs. Rini Tan the right to represent as "father" in the finalization of the adoption proceedings from this point on, and to have for herself the privilege of adopting said Eddy Ie Swieson as her son."

The group surrounding the wheelchair all nodded quickly, with some show of impatience.

"Now is it fully understood that once I have signed this document, Mrs. Rini Tan will be granted permanent rights – which cannot be regained – and this includes the right to represent herself as "father" as well as mother of the said Eddy Ie Swieson, and all other required privileges without exception, in order that she can be instrumental in bringing the adoption to finalization. For the record I should say that these adoption proceedings have been unduly delayed, having been begun in the year 1932 and, because of legal restrictions, civil disturbances and changes of government, have been held in abeyance, now, for – let's see – for 42 years!"

The group nodded impatiently.

"Then I will now sign this certificate, and the witnesses will also sign." There was silence for a moment, except for the sound of pens scratching on paper.

"Finally," the clerk said, drawing a deep breath, "I must also note for the record that the former father of Eddy Ie Swieson, due to paralysis and pain from severe rheumatism, has not been able to put his signature in writing. Therefore, his fingerprint appears on this document instead, along with witnessing signatures of Wenda Setijawati, Sri Woelan, and Soembono Tjiptowidjojo."

As the witnesses signed their names, the clerk erased his frown and flashed a quick official smile. "I now hand you the completed certificate to be mailed to Mrs. Rini Tan," he said. "I wish her well in her efforts to complete the adoption in as short a time as possible." He nodded a brisk "goodbye" and turned his attention to another pile of papers.

A tear rolled down the cheek of the crippled Indro Imanjaja as they wheeled him to the door, and one of the ladies wiped it off with her handkerchief. They all could imagine the thoughts that were passing through his mind at that moment. He had just relinquished all rights to call himself the father of a son he had abandoned to die at three weeks old, a son now well-known in Asia and in America.

Over and over again, in the years after Rini Tan had in her words, "scooped" me from the floor of a slum dwelling in Java, where I was near death, and rushed me to a clinic, she had applied for adoption papers. But there was always a formidable tangle of red tape, made virtually impassable by discriminatory practices against the Chinese. The revolutionary government required them even to abandon their Chinese names and re-register under Indonesian names. This complicated the adoption process, and for years made it impossible.

Year after year my foster mother, determined that I should be her "son" legally as well as in her heart, besieged the callous and unyielding Indonesian officials. The list of excuses for refusing her request grew long over the years, but there was always another excuse.

Meanwhile I had moved to the United States to become, first, a radio minister, and then associate pastor of one of Washington's largest churches. My renown as a Bible scholar had echoed back, even as far as the tropical Indonesian islands. This proud little Chinese lady insisted on calling herself my "mother" and kept coming back, again and again, to claim her right to adopt me.

In later years she gradually shed her subservient attitude before the Indonesian bureaucrats. She looked them right in the eyes, and told them what she wanted and what she thought about their excuses. After all, was she not the "mother" of Eddy Swieson? That, in her eyes and in the eyes of thousands of other Christians in Indonesia, made her "somebody special."

When my foster father passed away in the spring of 1973, the president of the Board of Fourth Presbyterian Church, Mr. H. Vance Chadwick, suggested that it might be a comfort for my mother in her grief to come to Washington to visit us and be with her young grandson, Dana.

The idea took hold. Plans were laid, and in June 1974 Mrs. Rini Tan arrived in Washington, D.C. There was a tearful, joyful meeting, then days and days of conversation when words tumbled over words as we caught up with the experiences of the past 12 years.

And, as might have been expected, the long, frustrated process of adoption was one of things we talked about. "I wonder if it is now too late," Rini said. "Your natural father is still alive, but very ill and partly paralyzed. He would have to sign. There would have to be court proceedings. They have refused so long. Do you think they might help us, now that you have so many friends here in America?"

Federal Judge Martin Bostetter Jr., a member of Fourth Church, stopped to talk to me on a Sunday soon afterward, and the question was put to him. "Would it be possible now to have the adoption made legal here in the United States?" Judge Bostetter thought there might be some delays and complications, but saw no reason why it could not be done. But he urged that action get under way immediately, when he learned that my father was so seriously ill.

So Judge Bostetter started the wheels turning, volunteering to prepare the legal papers to be sent to Indonesia. It was his legal help that finally led to the scene in the little courtroom in Mojokerto on September 18, 1974 when Indro Imanjaja (my natural father), paralyzed and in a wheelchair, unable to sign his name, put his fingerprint on the document by which he relinquished all rights to call himself the father of the baby he had abandoned as "dying" 42 years earlier.

Now the scene shifted to the Montgomery County Courthouse, in Rockville, Maryland. Judge Plummer M. Shearin presided over the final formalities of an adoption hearing. He looked over the papers and was told, in a whisper by an aide that "both parties are

Chinese, one an American citizen, the other still a resident and citizen of Indonesia."

With a gentle tap of the gavel, he called for me and Mrs. Rini Tan to come forward to the bench for a conference.

"This is a very unusual case," he remarked. "Why has there been this extraordinary delay? I understand that you, Dr. Swieson, are the son who is to be adopted, and that your mother, Mrs. Rini Tan, has been your foster mother, in fact, for all your life. And you are now 42 years old."

"Is this a matter of qualifying for an inheritance? Is there some money or property involved? Before I approve these adoption documents I would like to know what is behind it all. Could you tell me, now, what are your motives for wanting to be adopted by this woman at this late date?"

Trying to suppress a chuckle, I replied, "Certainly, your Honor. I will be glad to give you the story. There is no money motive. There is no inheritance that I know of – except the inheritance of good health and life itself, that this lady, whom I have always regarded as my real mother, already has given me."

Then I gave the judge a brief sketch of the miracles that God had permitted Rini Tan to perform in His name. I recounted her long struggle to have the adoption legalized, and the fears that she might never realize her dream to legally adopt one that was already her son in every way, except legally.

The judge finally raised a restraining hand and smilingly interrupted. "All right, I asked for it, and I think I got it. I can understand what you mean when you complain of legal red tape. So we'll put an end to the red tape delays right here and now." And to Rini Tan, he added, "Madam, I admire your determination and your wonderful success as a mother." With that, Judge Shearin signed the adoption document and handed it to her.

In early February 1975, weeks later than planned, Rini Tan said goodbye to me and my family and returned to her home in Java. In March 1975 – just one month later – my real father, Indro Imanjaja, quietly passed away in his home. The Lord had kept him alive just long enough to reward the brave little Chinese woman who had rescued and nurtured me for a fruitful life of service to the kingdom of God. ✞

Chapter 12

Perspective of the Indonesians

Looking back at Indonesia, from the perspective provided by so many years absence and 10,000 miles distance, I am reminded of what the Apostle Paul told the super-cautious people of Athens. As he walked past Mars Hill, he found an altar inscribed "To the Unknown God" standing in the midst of scores of altars honoring every pagan god known to mankind. So he gathered an audience of Athenians and told them, "Men of Athens, I notice that you are very religious." Then he told them he was there to testify about the unknown God "You have been worshipping without knowing who He is."

Indonesians today are doing what the Athenians did 2000 years ago. They are Muslim, animist, ancestor-worshiping, Buddhist, and Confucianists, for a starter. They are not only tolerant of all religions, but are inclined to accept and embrace some feature or features of every new religion that comes along. Their religion is probably the nearest approach to the worship of all gods without discrimination.

The job of today's missionary in Indonesia, therefore, is not to convince the people of the importance of worshiping God, but to prove to them the reality and the power of the one Almighty God and His Son, Jesus Christ. The Lord right now is working old-fashioned biblical-type miracles among the Indonesian people. Nothing less will save them from the deeply rooted pagan superstitions of many centuries past.

I witnessed some of these miracles, even though my ministry in Indonesia was very short. Some of these are described in these pages: the miracle of the stopping of a rainy season flood for the duration of a five-day Christian crusade in Java; the miraculous healing of my grandmother that won most of my immediate family to Christ, along with many of their friends; my Buddhist father's rescue from the door of death after a heart attack, when he allowed a Christian pastor to pray with him. My own survival from certain death in a Java slum at age of three weeks, and the events that led me to a Christian ministry in America, are undeniable miracles.

I believe that God will demonstrate His power through more such miracles, and even greater miracles. The time is late, and the time-tested missionary tactics tend to bounce off the friendly Indonesians. If you have a new god or a new doctrine and take it to Indonesia, the people there, like the men of Athens, might bow to your God and accept at least some of your new doctrine. They might add what they have taken, to their already complicated pantheon, and never discard any of the old gods or beliefs.

Indonesia is, indeed, a frustrating mission field. The missionary's chief problem is the same as the one faced by the old farmer. He was asked by a friend why every time he hitched his mules to the plow, he first delivered some stinging whacks to their hindquarters. "They're fine mules," the farmer answered, "and they do a fine job pulling the plow. But first, I have to get their undivided attention."

The missionary in Indonesia must draw the undivided attention of the Indonesians to the power and the love of Almighty God, to the exclusion of all their pagan gods. It's a great blessing when the Lord helps out with a miracle. I have tried to explain, in chapter four about my conversion, what drew me to Christ when, at 17, I first began to read the New Testament. What a contrast when compared with Buddhism, our family's religion at that time.

Buddhism offered an endless series of lives and deaths, and reincarnations to life, possibly different and less desirable. It was a terrifying future to me, as a youth, and I saw no escape. I feared death because of the uncertainty of what kind of a human or animal or even insect would be my lot the next time around.

What I wanted most in the whole world was a God who would give me peace of mind and spirit in this life. I was seeking a way to make amends for my sins in this life, so I would not be punished for them in the next life, by being reincarnated as one of the lower animals or insects.

I had reached a physically dangerous state of mental depression over my failure to find any such means of personal salvation. Then, by the grace of God, I was led to open the New Testament and read Paul's concise presentation of Christianity, the Good News that

Christ died to forgive our sins, and that if we accept Him by faith we have everlasting life, with only happiness beyond the grave.

It took a miracle to get that New Testament into my hands, and another to bring me to the point of spiritual desperation in which I was willing to do anything to escape my fate. At that point, I seemed to have done everything else. So I opened the Book and read about Christ.

There is a strange parallel between Buddhist doctrine and Christian doctrine – up to a point. The Buddhists say that man craves unworthy things. It is his nature to do so. And these things, they hold, defile his nature. The consequent defilement brings suffering, which leads to death. This death brings only a new start in life by the unceasing "wheel of rebirth" or reincarnation. Your level of life the next time around depends on the kind of life you led on your previous tour. The name for this is Karma, which means, to the Buddhist, that you reap what you sow.

Christian doctrine also warns that we reap what we sow, and that wages of sin is death. But at that point the two religions part company. For the Christian, sins are forgiven through faith in Jesus Christ, with the assurance of everlasting happiness and peace. Christianity is a positive, upbeat faith that offers answers and leaves no doubts.

The Apostle Paul put it succinctly in describing the pagan religions of his day. The philosophies of these other religions, he said, are but the shadow of what is to come. Christianity offers the Savior, Jesus Christ, the substance of what is to come. Christ is the difference!✝

Chapter 13

Perspective of the Americans

The United States has been my home since 1963. Since 1970 I have been an American citizen. I thank God for the opportunities, the freedom, and the comforts of my adopted homeland. Coming as a 30 year old my passion was to learn, not to criticize. Indeed, I have studiously refrained from criticizing, but in my work as a pastor for over 30 years, I have had opportunities to watch the American scene at close range. My background as an educated Asian may have made it possible for me to discern some trends, and possibly some dangers that Americans might miss because of their long familiarity with things as they are.

Some things are obvious, e.g. the defiance of our youth, the over-emphasis on sexual freedom, the widening gap between the haves and the have-nots, the diminishing religious inheritance of the Americans, caused by the growing legion of religious "drop-outs." We all know these trends exist, and most of us hope they are temporary, that they will pass with time.

But in my years here, I have been watching a trend that, to my Asian mind, seems even more destructive and diabolical. This new, growing danger imperils the very existence of American society. It is destroying human sensitivity, ruining human relationships, and suffocating much that is fine in our lives.

It is alarming that most of us are unaware of this increasing peril, and many even hail it with enthusiasm as an admirable and acceptable trend. I am speaking of the growing pressures and the increasing "speed" being built into the sophisticated American way of life. Americans in general do not have the time to do all they apparently want to do, so they are rushing through life without taking the time to savor the joys, benefits, and satisfactions this great country offers.

Moreover, this acceleration of American life has been devastating to millions of families. These are the foundations on which our civilization was built. Divorce rates are soaring, multiple marriages are commonplace. There is little time reserved for home life.

We all know the picture all around us. As we see so much of it, we are accepting it as normal. Believe me, it is not normal. The Devil would like nothing better than to turn us away from the wise course charted by our godly forefathers.

We are developing a throw-away society, which considers it harmful and wasteful to slow down, because it would hurt business and industry. People are being conditioned by the pressures toward ever-faster production, and ever-faster consumption to keep up with the production. As production and consumption vie to exceed each other in the soaring upward spiral, little attention is being paid to human beings, who live in the roaring vortex of these economic cyclones. The human element in this mindless system is heading toward collapse.

Many children, asking for attention, a little affection, or help with their studies, are brushed aside. Faced with mounting bills, housewives and mothers, in fast-growing numbers, are abandoning their God-given privileges and taking jobs and joining the "rat-race." The computer which started as our servant, is fast becoming our master, telling us what to do and when to do it, relieving us of the need to "think."

Could it be that the current wave of youthful rebellion and defiance grew out of resentment at being ignored by their enterprising, aggressive parents? Could it be that the growing crime wave among our youth was born of bitter misunderstanding between parents and children, a misunderstanding that had its roots in lack of time to get acquainted?

The breathless speed of life, the lack of time even to think, will eventually draw a dividing line through all of humanity, not only the American family. This might trigger misunderstanding and bitterness between Main Street and Wall Street, men and women, East and West. It has the potential to destroy us.

But as Americans, we not only condone the system that could destroy us, we praise the ultra-fast life as "the American way." We pour out fortunes that we earn with such speed, buying *instant* coffee and *instant* food, which gives us *instant* indigestion for which various remedies are *instant* cures. We push for *instant* travel, in faster and faster airplanes, even if it means *instant* death. Television and radio offer us *instant* entertainment, or *instant* boredom and vulgarity.

Now we are seeing a new development: *instant* political reform by assassination, bombing, and indiscriminate terrorist attacks. How can humanity survive if the best of us lack conviction and compassion, and the worst are full of passionate intensity and self-seeking? We have abandoned rationality when we talk of *instant* perception and production. Do we really believe that our minds think faster now than they did in pre-electronic times?

It is essential to remind ourselves that we live in a world that is spiritual as well as physical. Christians, especially, must keep this constantly in mind. God's Word in Ecclesiastes 3 tells us that for everything there is a time and a season, a time for every matter under heaven.

Jesus was ever conscious of the divine pace. He never tried to hurry or accelerate God's timing. He moved carefully and consciously according to the divine schedule. He even waited for human maturity before starting His ministry. After His exciting dialogue with the scribes and doctors in the Temple, as a youth, He waited another 18 years, until He was 30, before starting His teaching ministry.

The accelerating pace of our lives is dulling our sensitivity to the Creator, eroding our sense of responsibility to our fellow-humans.

My father, after becoming a Christian, told me that he found great similarity between the wisdom of the Book of Ecclesiastes and the teachings of the ancient Chinese philosopher, Confucius. Both advise the human family to maintain a happy balance in their lives, a balance between action and recreation, between attention to family and attention to others in need, and between silence and conversation.

The Bible carries the admonition further. God tells us to reserve a time for living beyond the immediate and situational. We must have a vision of eternity in order to bring our lives into proper focus. We must be willing to *move with the rhythm of God.*

Listen to the solemn words of Jesus, "You are the salt of the earth. But what good is salt if it has lost its flavor? Can you make it salty again? It will be thrown out and trampled underfoot as worthless. You are the light of the world – like a city on a hilltop that cannot be hidden. No one lights a lamp and then puts it under a basket. Instead, a lamp is placed on a stand, where it gives light to everyone in the house.

In the same way, let your good deeds shine out for all to see, so that everyone will praise your heavenly Father." (Matthew 5:13-16, NLT).

Footnote from Eddy: How amazing and alarming that I wrote this chapter 35 years ago, It is so accurate and relevant today in 2010! The Internet has entered the scene - accelerating these trends. Our only hope for restoring our American historical values is in a mighty work of God. ✝

Chapter 14

Epilogue – The Past 35 Years

As the proverbial saying goes: "There is an appointed time for everything" (Ecclesiastes 3:1,NAS).

In 1980 Dr. Halverson left his position as senior pastor of Fourth Presbyterian Church to assume a new position in the Capitol as the United States Senate Chaplain.

Once more, I faced a major challenge. Our denomination, the Presbyterian Church (U.S.A.), has a firm policy prohibiting any associate minister to be nominated as a senior pastor in that same congregation.

Even before Dr. Halverson left, I was advised by close friends to move on also. Here is the reasoning for such a suggestion. Since my long-standing ministry to so many Fourth Church members had created a close bond, it could create an awkward if not a difficult situation for the new pastor, for me to stay at Fourth.

I took the counsel seriously. In the summer of 1982, when the Pastoral Search Committee of Fourth Church called a new pastor, I became the founding pastor of a new congregation in Rockville, Maryland. This was God's answer to my unceasing longing to know and serve every member in a congregation.

While radio broadcasting was an exciting endeavor, with over three million people listening regularly, I did not have the joy of meeting them face-to-face. Likewise, my ministry at the large and growing Fourth Church was a wonderful experience, yet so often I lamented inwardly for being unable to help everyone in that 2000 member congregation.

Working with the leadership of Community Bible Study for five years, I observed how the leaders could care for their large size classes of between 200 to 300 participants, by developing small groups with a core-leader for each. There was a burning desire in my heart to develop a congregation in that manner. So I accepted the call by a group of Christians in Rockville. Daily I asked God for His grace and wisdom to serve every person He sent to this new body of believers. It was known as Christian Covenant Church, a non-denominational community congregation.

With the support and eager willingness of my wife, Debbie, we in time invited each individual or couple to come for lunch or dinner in our home. Our desire was to get to know them personally.

124

When people needed counseling, I offered to meet in a café near their workplace, wherever that might be. Such an approach surprised many, and at the same time gave me the utmost joy to know even where they work. I don't remember ever asking the board for a pastor's office in the building. I normally followed up each visit with a handwritten note, including a prayer.

As the congregation began to grow and young people joined their parents to worship on Sunday mornings, God sent us a wonderful, dynamic young minister, Greg Zetts, who shared my philosophy of ministry. His frequent presence with them as well as his genuine love for them was magnetic. Scores of young people flocked to his teaching sessions. They dedicated their lives to Christ and His mission, to help the needy in Maryland as well as in Mexico. Greg even took them to India, Vietnam, and Guatemala.

Even one of our County Police Departments asked Greg to serve as chaplain. So we got more as a congregation than we had expected. We remained close knit and healthy spiritually and financially to the time I left them in the fall of 1997, when I reached 65. The church board unanimously called Greg Zetts to be their senior pastor.

Before Debbie and I departed for San Diego, where we would make our new residence, friends from the church planned a lavish retirement party. It was a moving experience for Debbie and me as we saw so many gathered in the large reception room of Fourth Church. Thirty-two years of ministry in two congregations naturally drew many faithful friends, and quite a number of Fourth Church members were present.

Many tears were shed, as one by one they shared their blessed experience through the grace of God. One of the speakers asked the people, "How many of you during Dr. Swieson's pastoral ministry have received personal, hand-written notes from him? Please raise your hands." To our surprise, everyone raised his or her hand. This was followed by long applause. In tears I thanked God for giving me His love and discipline to touch for Him, on a consistent basis the people He sent to me.

I only wished my mother, who died in 1987, and Dr. Halverson, who died in 1995, could have been with us to witness the fruits of their labors of love towards us.

Having received so many blessings from God, and so much love from people in my adopted land of America, there burned in my heart a deep longing to give back the same love through any service I could render to God and country.

Another inspiration which touched me strongly before I left the pastorate was the revelation Jesus shared with His early followers in Matthew, "You are the world's light...Let it shine for all; let your good deeds glow for all to see, so that they will praise your heavenly Father" (Matt. 5:14, 16 LB). That statement refers to the very life of Christ in us, which must be actualized in the environment where we live and work everyday, and not be confined within the four walls of the church. That's the reason upon my retirement that I desired to put into practice the appeal of our Lord to all of us to live as His "living Bibles" at home and in the marketplace.

Finally, in early October 1997, Debbie and I bade farewell to our family to fly to San Diego, our new hometown. Our hearts were saddened at the same time because we would be 3000 miles from our only child, Dana, and his family who were living in Philadelphia, PA. Dana met his future wife, Lisa Roth, from Fairfield,

CT, while both of them studied at the University of Pennsylvania. They now have two boys, Caleb and James, and two girls, Julia and Xing Hua. Dana is a mechanical engineer, and operates his own business that deals with energy purchasing. Lisa has taken a very courageous step by home-schooling all four children through high school. She has done a remarkable job. The two boys are now attending universities, for which they have earned scholarships.

What pleases us most, is the fact that they all love the Lord, and are very active in their churches. Dana is serving as an Elder at Springton Lake Presbyterian Church (PCA) in Newtown Square, PA where they live. I'm confident that by now Dana has forgiven me for letting him, as an infant, struggle in his mother's womb on April 13, 1965, without my sympathy and presence in the delivery room of Suburban hospital in Bethesda, Maryland. As you may recall, this happened because of my skeptical opinion that he might be born in April, instead of in May as the doctor foretold. Indeed, I deserved that severe chastisement from one of the senior staff at Fourth Church because of my seeming lack of compassion. I promised Dana and his family that we would call them at least once a week from our new home in California, and also try to visit them every year.

As we began to settle in our new home in Carlsbad near San Diego, I shared with Debbie what was on my heart, just to make sure that we were on the same wave-length. Here is what I told her: "From now on I want to offer my God-given talents and time for the good of many around us in the spirit of volunteerism. For many years the good Lord has showered us with countless blessings, our adopted country which has provided us freedom to grow, and friends to support us when we needed help."

Soon after we settled in our new home, I received a phone call from someone who knew me and my ministry to professional and business people in the Washington, D.C. area. Here in San Diego he was the leader of a men's group that regularly met at Rancho Santa Fe Country Club for prayer and study of the Scripture. Having heard that I was living in his area, he offered me the opportunity to share some biblical teachings with the group. About 30 men, mostly churchgoers, attended the meeting.

With their consent, I shared with them the biblical concept of being in the marketplace for the glory of God. From the beginning I impressed upon their minds not to separate the secular from the sacred, by showing how the Lord Jesus lived and worked when He was on earth.

I made it clear from the Gospel records how Jesus did not confine Himself or His work to the synagogue, or the temple in Jerusalem. Our Lord mingled with people who were at work, whether in a fishing boat on the Sea of Galilee, or on land with the farmers. He blessed the laborers to cause their efforts to be productive. In fact, on several occasions Jesus spoke on the subject of what today we call, "financial growth" by using parables of the talents and diligent stewardship. I also pointed out how the Apostle Paul in like manner appealed to his fellow-Christians to consider that whatever they did, they should work at it with all their hearts, for they were working for Christ (Colossians 3:23-24).

Another important concept which I sought to impress upon their minds was, "Be sure there is a correlation between what we profess among fellow Christians and how we live in the marketplace." The idea that they as professional and business people could be in the service of God, through their daily and personal consecration to God, excited them beyond description. They began to ask me to visit with them in their respective workplaces, and to pray not just for them, but also for their associates and clients. It is thrilling for me to learn how one of them began to pray for the drivers who drove the vehicles that would be sold from the dealership he owned. When I asked, "How do you know which car was sold from your dealership?" The answer was obvious; "I recognize it from the logo on the frame around the license plate."

While with the group, aside from giving them inspiration from God's Word, I maintained close contact with each one by sending them personal notes or phoning them. When one of them became ill or was hospitalized I tried to be at his bedside right away.

During one of those visits to Scripps Memorial Hospital, I met one of the hospital's directors, who had heard of my 32 years of pastoral and counseling experience in Washington, D.C. The next time she saw me, she asked whether I would be willing to assist them by providing spiritual care service to some of their patients, especially those who were going through rehabilitation. At that time the hospital did not have an official position of chaplain. I accepted the offer on a volunteer basis. What gave me the utmost joy in this capacity was to experience the pleasant surprises that came through my encounters with some of the patients.

One morning as I was visiting a patient and sharing a brief devotional with her from my little Bible, the lady in the next bed greeted me as I was about to leave. When I responded to her greetings, and walked toward her bed, she said to me: "I heard you praying from the book of Psalms, and you used some Hebrew words. I am Jewish and belong to the Knesset in Israel. I became ill during my visit here. Perhaps I ate something that didn't agree with me. Have you been to Israel and do you speak Hebrew?"

Without hesitation I responded, "Yes, indeed. I have made at least seven study tours in your country. In fact, because of my interest in your Bible, I spent a couple of years attending a Hebrew conversational class in one of the Jewish Community Centers in Washington, D.C."

She began to smile. Then she admitted to me, that she did not expect to hear a Chinese using Hebrew words, and in addition showing such genuine interest in her Jewish culture. I was absolutely thrilled when she told me: "In the future when you revisit my country, be sure to give me a call. My name is listed in the Knesset. I would like to give you a personal tour through our Parliament building." I was dumbfounded. Then she continued, "Before you leave, would you mind praying for me?"

Still overwhelmed by her generosity and confidence in me, I reached out to hold her hands and began to pray. By this time I was almost choked up with joyful emotion. As usual, I recited a couple of God's promises from the Old Testament to preface my prayer. At the conclusion of my petition when we bade farewell, she was drenched with tears.

All the way home from the hospital I was praising and thanking God for reaching out to one of His own people!

In June 1999, when San Diego International Airport was seeking for an airport volunteer to assist the traveling public, I submitted an application to the Director of Customer Service, who was happy to sign me up. Since aviation was one of my passions, which I mentioned during the interview, he immediately sent me to an orientation class. The following week he provided me with the required official airport badge. I figured that by devoting two or three days weekly at the San Diego International Airport, I could still keep up with my other commitments.

When the tragic event of September 11, 2001 occurred, this produced major disruption in airports everywhere, as many of my readers will remember. I volunteered to assist the airlines and airport authority to monitor and record the movements of confused passengers around ticket counters and security check points. At that time the Transportation Security Administration (TSA) was not yet operating in our airports. On a regular basis at the end of my workday, I submitted a typewritten report to the airport authority, in which I identified the problems and suggested possible solutions.

Copies of my reports were further conveyed to airlines managers. Soon they invited me to attend their monthly Lindbergh Airport Managers Council, during which from time to time the chairman asked me to give an oral report. Meanwhile, some officials of the airport authority collected my data, and used it to help undertake improvements in crucial locations where most passengers converged for security. The following year when the TSA under the U.S. Homeland Security was introduced to San Diego International Airport, copies of my bi-weekly reports were also sent to their office.

Although it has not been an easy routine to be on the job at the airport at 5:00 a.m. two or three times a week, I have enjoyed every minute serving in those challenging and busy terminals. An airport official once described my job as being "a happy consultant without pay."

One day one of the airline managers with whom I had worked closely invited me to come with him to Phoenix International Airport, where he was going on business. To my surprise, he introduced me to several airport officials, telling them what I had been doing in San Diego. They gave me a tour of the airport, which was much larger than San Diego International Airport. The tour gave me some even better ideas on how to make airline passengers less apprehensive when going through the security process.

On a few occasions during my intense activities, I had the joy of identifying friends from the Washington, D.C. area who were flying from the San Diego airport. One of the pleasant surprises was when I recognized the gentleman who was sitting in a wheelchair, waiting to be processed at our security checkpoint. It was the former U.S. Surgeon General, Dr. C. Everett Koop. At that point I made an extra effort to meet him in the departure lounge, and I was deeply touched by his sweet smile as he recognized me. We had a good visit, reminiscing about the mutual blessings we had experienced at Fourth Church. In the past while visiting Fourth, Dr. Koop had given us very helpful, well-balanced teaching on health, based on biblical principles. That morning before he was wheeled onto the aircraft, we prayed together for God's continuing support and strength.

A week later, I received from our beloved Dr. Koop a very thoughtful, personal note, mentioning how immensely impressed he was by the fine service at San Diego International Airport. After reading the letter, I simply couldn't keep it to myself. The next day I showed Dr. Koop's letter to one of the airport authority officials to whom I was accountable. He too was touched by the content, and asked whether he could relay it to the members of the Executive Board of the airport, because he wanted the CEO to see it. We were delighted that a former high-ranking U.S. government official would offer such a generous compliment to our airport in San Diego.

When I first began ministry at Fourth Church, I felt a certain apprehension due to my own more retiring temperament. Would I be able to measure up to such an overwhelming and important responsibility and opportunity? God proved sufficient by supplying me with wisdom, strength, and courage for the work to which He called me. I felt similar awe and apprehension about whether I could meet the expectations of the government officials. Although my position was voluntary, I had never worked for the United States government before. However, this too was a service as unto the Lord, and I did my best to be God's representative in a secular situation in the marketplace.

Once again, God proved faithful. Wonder of wonders, one day I received an invitation to attend a ceremony at the airport to be hosted by the Department of Homeland Security, the Transportation Security Administration. To my great surprise, I saw my name listed in the program as one of the award recipients!

Before the director of the TSA, General Michael Aguilar, handed the decorative plaque to me, he read it aloud: "Volunteer of the Year award 2004, presented to Dr. Eddy Swieson in appreciation of your outstanding service and commitment to TSA." The audience response was spontaneous, and the roar of applause filled the auditorium. In my heart, once more, I thanked God for enabling me to contribute an important service to my adopted country.

To those who suggest that I might be taking on too much in my retirement for the good of my health, I normally reply with gentle tolerance, "God never gives us more than we can do; He always gives us time and energy to do it." Although I may have attained the closest human approach to perpetual motion, I feel blessed to be always conscious of the presence of the Lord, including when I am driving on the Freeway to the airport at 4:00 in the morning.

At home, when I do pause from my activities, I make myself listen to God by reading the Scripture in other languages, such as German, Greek and Chinese, rather than reading my familiar English Bible. In fact, during the past two years I have been hand-copying both the Greek and German New Testaments. What inspiring insights I have gained through such a discipline!

Speaking of discipline, realizing that we are not getting younger physically, Debbie and I have promised the Lord that we would keep our bodies in good shape by nourishing them with healthy food. Our regular diet generally consists of fish and chicken, with plenty of vegetables. Instead of enjoying desserts after our meals, we consume a lot of fruit. Thanks to living in California, we have no shortage of delicious fresh fruit even during the winter season. Our primary physician, who stresses preventive health care, has also recommended plenty of vitamin supplements for us.

After all, we believe that these bodies are the "sanctuaries" of the Spirit of God; hence it is our responsibility to be good stewards by taking care of them well. That includes our daily exercise, which consists of swimming and brisk walking every day.

It has been my desire since I retired from the pastorate to give myself wholeheartedly to serve our adopted country as long as God provides the strength and ability to do so. Indeed, it is in gratitude to God and to this beloved nation that we are serving Him together!✝

"Now we know why the angels at last are laughing WITH JOY.

Although death meant to steal away my life before it even got started, God meant it for good. As the Scripture tells us, 'Everything that happens fits into a pattern for good.'

God destined my aunt to rescue and nurture me and give my life direction. Then He gave me Debbie, my beautiful wife, to serve with me. That set our course in life, and for these many years God has used us in His service.

As it was with Caleb, who was known to 'follow the Lord wholeheartedly' all the days of his life, we are still doing so, as long as our God gives us breath!"

To God be the Glory!
